The Marriage Workout Book

For Anna and Olivia Kirk

The Marriage Work-Out Book

Mary Kirk

Published by
Lion Publishing plc
Sandy Lane West, Oxford, England
ISBN 0 7459 3352 1
Albatross Books Pty Ltd
PO Box 320, Sutherland, NSW 2232, Australia
ISBN 0 7324 1314 1

First edition 1996
10 9 8 7 6 5 4 3 2 1 0

A catalogue record for this book is available
from the British Library

Printed and bound in Great Britain
by Cox & Wyman Ltd, Reading

Acknowledgments

I am extremely grateful to
Dr Liberty Kovacs of the Center
for Marriage and Family
Therapy, Sacramento CA, for
making her work available to
me, and to Dr Deirdre Morrod
of One Plus One, the marriage
and partnership research
charity. My gratitude also and
as ever goes to Dr Jack
Dominian and to Ann Lawson
for all they have taught me. I
should like to thank my
researcher,
David Kitton, without whom
this book would have been
impossible. Numerous exercise
and workout tapes and books
were consulted, and any
aerobics terms used are an
amalgam of all of these. My
thanks go to Marriage Care
(formerly CMAC, the Catholic
Marriage Advisory Council)
counsellors who provided case
material and were ready to
help and advise. I am grateful
too to the many couples who
allowed me into their lives to
interview them. I am also
obliged to Eileen McCabe of
Marriage Care whose particular
interest in the stages of moral
development was one of the
springboards for this book.
Finally I should like to record
how much I owe to many
others encountered along the
journey of relationships.
Mary Kirk, July 1995

Contents

Foreword

This book could not be more timely. The passage of the Family Law Bill, 1996, replacing the 1969 Divorce Law, has focussed attention on the importance of 'reflection and consideration' when one partner in a marriage believes that the marriage has irretrievably broken down. Mary Kirk has drawn from a wealth of sources, sociological research, the findings of modern psychology, contemporary journalism and the experiences of couples in counselling (ensuring, of course, that they cannot be identified) to invite us to reflect on and consider the whole of marriage. She engages us on the journey of development that every marriage can be, and sets us challenges: shall we climb the ladder to the next stage or slip down the ever-present snake?

Rightly described as a work-out book, it does not make false promises or provide facile how-to solutions. Many readers will recognize their own experience and see it in a new light as they go through the text. I trust that they will also perceive the encouragement to value their own resources in arriving at a desirable level of marriage 'fitness'. The mundane and the ordinary are as much the stuff of marriage as are the dramatic and exclusive intimacies—they all have the possibility for the individual partners in the marriage to be more truly themselves as well as building the couple's identity.

Mary Kirk's own training has uniquely equipped her to write this special book. It celebrates the reality and the potentiality of marriage: it promises hope. I know it will be of help to all who 'work out'. It deserves the widest distribution.

Mary Corbett
Chief Executive
Marriage Care

Introduction

Lynn and Vic met on a skiing holiday and discovered they were
from the same town in Essex. They had a lot to talk about and
quickly developed an intense relationship which included sex
from the start, despite the fact that Lynn came from a church-
going Baptist background. Lynn became pregnant and they
decided to marry quickly. During the course of the wedding
preparations Lynn found out that Vic had lied to her by saying
that he, too, was a committed Baptist, and—worse—that he had
already been married and divorced. All of a sudden reality
replaced romance for Lynn. Despite her doubts, the wedding
went ahead and the baby was born. More and more lies
emerged, and Lynn became ill, withdrawn and depressed. The
man she thought she had married did not exist. Her mother was
urging her to leave him. Vic was distraught. They were at an
impasse and there were bitter rows. They agreed to see a
counsellor.

We shall return to their story later.

If we're not changing we're dead.

You and I are not the same people we were ten years ago.
Although some people's emotional development is rapid and
spectacular, and others' is painfully slow and barely perceptible,
it nonetheless happens, as surely as we grow as children and
develop characteristics which belong to our gender or are
inherited through our genes, as surely as we age from one year
to the next.

So it is, too, with close relationships. If a couple's marriage or
partnership is not evolving, if it is stuck where and how it was
years ago, then it may become moribund, like a pot-bound
plant, and die if not rescued.

Another way of looking at a relationship is to say that for it to
grow and change it needs exercise and hard work. We have to

be able to recognize how fit our marriage is, and be committed to keeping it in shape. As those workout videos tell us, 'You don't get the best body you can by wishing for it—you *can* get it by work.' A close relationship is the same. It is something worked at and sweated for over the years; it will not just happen because we are in love. Yet before we can even begin to work at a relationship, we have to understand and accept who we are, and how we have become the way we are.

Children's physical growth is determined by a myriad of different factors: genes, diet, environment, nurture and often the care the mother took during pregnancy. So, also, the development of our personality is affected by many influences: who our parents were and how they responded to parenthood, how they were treated as children, the number of brothers and sisters we have, traumatic events during childhood and—perhaps above all—whether the amount of love and security we were given in our earliest years matched the amount we needed. Sometimes, when something vital was missing from the formative times of our upbringing we can arrest at that particular emotional stage, until someone, somewhere, later helps us complete that part of our growth.

Our emotional development as children will programme our behaviour for the rest of our lives. It will guide us—or in times of stress or pain push us hard—towards one decision and away from another; it will determine how we act and react in different situations; it will play a large part in unconsciously pre-determining the mate we select. But our mate, our partner, our spouse, will also have been moulded and shaped by his or her family, environment, nurture and life events, and so from the depths of our childhood we come to each other to form a partnership. The interaction of two people in intimate relation-ship is a jungle of tangled influences, in which their individual growth and change must somehow enable a separate entity—the couple—to be born, to evolve and to develop.

Because of this, a marriage or committed couple relationship can seem more like a game of snakes and ladders than a smooth and well-choreographed workout. We set out together in confidence and hope, determined to throw the right dice, and to move smoothly onwards together through life. But the snakes are there, waiting to swallow us down—the huge serpents of jealousy, inability to communicate, craving for affection and attention, of controlling behaviour, lack of trust, dependence, of family patterns, defences, gender differences, of sexual difficulties, of high expectations and low performance, of anger and depression, and of fear of abandonment. There are also the smaller snakes of irritating habits, thoughtlessness, fatigue, financial problems, worries over children or ageing relatives, job insecurity, and so on.

Yet marriage is something most still yearn for, and Britain has one of the highest marriage rates in Europe. Although the numbers of those taking the vow have dropped, nearly 60 per cent in Britain will be married at some time. The rise in long-term cohabitation modelled on marriage suggests that the majority of people seek to live their adult lives in partnership. Even when one marriage does not work out, we are willing to have another go. In 1990, 36 per cent of all marriages were remarriages, witnessing to the triumph of hope over experience. Although it is predicted that by the end of the century four out of ten new marriages will end in divorce, we do not often reflect that this implies that *six* in every ten couples do remain together, and that these partnerships are usually 'good enough', slipping down some snakes, to be sure, but also climbing ladders, changing, growing.

Marriage can be health-giving and life-enhancing. It can be fun going up ladders together, meeting each other's needs, and it can be gratifying when we manage to avoid a familiar snake or help steer our partner clear of it, moving on through the squares of self-awareness and communication. But how do we cope if one of us keeps landing on the same snake and just can't move on—or alternatively if one of us suddenly manages to go up a couple of ladders leaving our partner, wounded and betrayed at being left behind, languishing in the square where they've been for years?

This book is about couples in relationship rather than the two individuals. It is an offering to those, like Vic and Lynn, whose dice appear loaded against them. It is for those who seem constantly to repeat the same patterns, landing on the same snakes, never moving on, but going back down and round again and again, trapped in low-grade, unfulfilling relationships, perhaps seeking to get off the board altogether. These are people who have been poorly served by the models they have observed in their earlier lives, and for whom it may seem impossible to live with their first choice of mate for ever.

The intention is to help people understand what is happening in their relationships; to recognize and accept their own personality—why they act and take decisions in a certain way and what the consequences of these may be on the partnership; to show how change can come about; and to see how this affects the growth of the marriage. Each step of relationship, each square of the board, with its niggles, tensions and crises, offers either a snake to channel us down ways we know only too well and where we've 'been there, done that, worn out the tee-shirt,' or a potential ladder to growth, helping us complete what has been missing in our development from childhood.

Not only do human beings change and grow in their bodies, minds, thoughts and feelings, but relationships also progress through stages. These stages are observable in almost any close relationship: first, that with our parents; then primarily in marriage or the committed couple relationship; and thirdly, in other family relationships, and in friendships, employment and organizations such as clubs, committees or the church.

The word 'stage' suggests—in this competitive world where we grew up and now live, move and have our being—that we *should* be aspiring to move ever onward and upward, that we *ought* always to be progressing. That is unreal and as depressing as being told we must all have beautiful aerobically fit bodies. We are conditioned to believe that 'getting to the top' (of the class, of the promotion ladder, of the league table) has a high value in the eyes of the world and that our own worth will increase the higher we climb. In terms of personality development, however, there is no judgment inherent in being at one point or another of our developmental journey, just as it is not necessarily better to be sixty than twenty, or to celebrate a silver

12

wedding anniversary rather than a first. These periods are different, not worse or better.

A deep relationship will usually start with an intensity which brings down the barriers between two people, excludes the rest of the world and precludes any caution or scepticism. We have our head in the clouds, everything is wonderful, we live for the other, dependent on his or her presence. Romance rules. But sooner or later a clearer vision replaces the rosy glow, and we begin to see more of the reality of the loved one (or friend or organization). There can follow a period of intense vying to see who will dominate, whose way will win, who is going to hold the reins of power within the relationship. There may then be a time when the partners step back and away from each other, trying to make sense of their life, who they are, where they are and why. We want to discover our true self and become that person. Separate interests may be pursued, and sometimes infidelity will result. Independence and maybe freedom are sought. In order for the relationship to survive, with our integrity intact, these differences must be negotiated and reconciled with respect for both partners' true selves. If this can be achieved, this relationship of two beings—together yet able to be separate, interdependent rather than clinging or straying, selfless rather than selfish—will survive, leaner and fitter, and be richly rewarding.

But relationships do get stuck at certain points, for within the couple there are two individuals with differing needs, backgrounds, outlooks and wounds to be healed; they themselves may be at different points on their own psychological and emotional journeys. There will inevitably arise times of conflict because of this, for conflict is part of relationship, the unavoidable concomitant of being together and trying to balance our availability to the other and our own needs. There used to be awarded, in Essex, something called the 'Dunmow Flitch'—a side of bacon given to the couple who could claim not to have had a row during their first year of marriage. But perfect peace is not the result of a living relationship—it is an inscription found on tombstones, and we sometimes need a pinch in order to be alive to the possibilities of change and growth.

Couples who think that quarrels are the end of the world, or at least of their life together, and who find it difficult to handle conflict, can take heart: rows are the moments in a relationship where a significant breakthrough becomes possible. In other words, when the dice fall on the 'conflict' square it can mean a ladder rather than a snake.

There is no prescription for idyllic happiness, no magic solution that will ensure living happily ever after—no one does. One counsellor said:

This is about struggle and conflict, this is about becoming real and becoming whole. Reality is not never having to say you're sorry.

Those who claim to have the perfect marriage may be protecting themselves against the sort of self-awareness which is as necessary to emotional growth as daylight is to a plant's growth. What this book attempts to do is to help those in relationships towards an awareness of what is happening to them on their pilgrim path together, to enable them to understand themselves and their partnerships better, and recognize all the defences, masks and ploys we use in our interaction with each other. Many people in relationship difficulties turn to counselling for help, but many others, even at crisis point, will never do so—for multiple reasons. This book, in its invitation to awareness of self and relationship, tries to be the counsellor on the bookshelf, facilitating change and growth before crisis is reached.

The book is divided into three sections.

The first part looks generally at marriage and those committed relationships that are, in the main, modelled on marriage. This section is a brief survey of what marriage is—both dream and reality, and of why the gap between these can be so great that people decide to part. It explores why we marry, and why we divorce. The second chapter of this first part investigates how we choose our mate and why, the psychological and largely unconscious reasons for this and how these cause us to interact with our partner. We look at the process of getting to know our partner so that when reality replaces romance it is not the beginning of the end but rather the end of the beginning. We see some of the defences and masks we all employ in order to survive every day, but which can hamper our efforts to be fully available emotionally to our partner—for, undefended by our habitual strategies we may feel too vulnerable to be ourselves.

The second part explores how our personality develops through a series of stages which, dependent on what happens to us as children, make us—emotionally and morally—the people we are.

The third and final part of this book looks at how to keep the relationship moving along the 'squares' of the 'board' of life together. Under stress or in times of crisis we all regress, both individually and as couples, to earlier points in our development. When trouble hits us, we may want to cling, be comforted, babied, nurtured. Often a couple will have to come back and 'redo' stages. Partners who spend significant periods apart, perhaps because work or illness takes them away, may find they have to start from square one again when they get back together—even though it may only take a few hours or days to progress through romance and reality to power struggle and a desire for independence and autonomy—and then negotiate their *modus vivendi* once more.

We explore the structure of quarrelling and moving apart, and how to avoid getting to the point where we want to call it quits. We also discuss the necessity for in-depth communication between partners as a way of avoiding the crunch.

Knowing what is going on can sometimes be a breakthrough when we are going through a bad patch. Similarly, knowing that others have the same experience and yet manage to have durable, 'good enough' marriages—where decisions can be taken together, and needs can be met and healing take place, and which as a result are empowering, energizing and enriching—can help take the sting out of feelings of isolation and despair when things go wrong. Because it is helpful to know of others' experience, I have included real-life stories of couples as they move through their relationships, with all the pain and gain that this can involve.

Much of the case material used in the book was provided by Marriage Care (formerly known as CMAC, the Catholic Marriage Advisory Council). This organization, which celebrates its golden jubilee in 1996, has pioneered counselling which focuses primarily on the relationship, while caring for both the couple and the individual; many other counselling agencies have tended to concentrate more on the individuals within a relationship. Marriage Care sees couples of every age, faith and culture, and has thus been able to furnish examples from many different backgrounds. In addition to this case material, the author has drawn on her own interviews with couples in both counselling and research. In all cases the names have been changed, and—where necessary—circumstantial detail has also been altered in order to safeguard confidentiality without distorting the case. No one is recognizable by his or her name, though it is inevitable that our fictitious names will have real-life namesakes. These are purely coincidental.

One other source of case and background material for this book has been newspapers and magazines, picked up at random, mainly during the months of preparation in late 1994 and early 1995 though some date back further. If interest by the press is an indicator of the public mind and heart, then marriage is not going out of fashion. Indeed, the flurry of articles at this time questioning the future of marriage suggests, by sheer quantity alone, that marriage is still of intense significance.

To love and be loved so that, despite failings, each is the most precious person in the world to the other, even after forty or fifty years, can be the highest of human achievements and the greatest of satisfactions. Marriage then matters most importantly because it is a statement that we, as individuals, matter.[1]

The theory of the developmental stages of the marriage journey was first formulated in this way by Dr Liberty Kovacs, who founded the Center for Marriage and Family Therapy in Sacramento, California, and much of the theoretical material in this book was made available by Dr Kovacs. This model has also been used by Dr Deirdre Morrod, training officer of One Plus One, the marriage and partnership research charity, and it was she who created the diagram of the stages in Chapter 5.

This is not an academic book, nor does it attempt to give an exhaustive picture of marriage. The subject of the book is the process of marriage and the journey of the couple themselves, and for this reason it does not include, except in passing, any reference to parenthood.

To avoid the use of non-inclusive language (the masculine personal pronoun and adjective applied to both men and women) and the clumsiness of saying 'him/her' all the time I have used the inclusive plural pronoun and adjective, though some readers may be uncomfortable with this as grammatically incorrect.

We return to the case of Lynn and Vic.

In counselling Vic's difficult background emerged. He had been in a children's home, was often in trouble, and had lacked affection and warmth. He had left school at fifteen, and worked hard, eventually to run his own computer company. Lynn, from her middle-class background, had seemed everything he wanted, and he had invented stories in order to win her, and also to escape from the grim reality of his own inadequacies, as he saw them. But he also needed tenderness which, because of her hurt and her suspicions, Lynn now could not give.

In the security of counselling Vic was able to move from his childish fantasy world to face reality as he had never done before. He set an agenda for change, knowing that he must accept the things that could not be altered. In time, some of his fantasies became reality, for he was converted to Christianity and became a member of the Baptist Church. As more time passed Vic became far more the person Lynn thought she had married, having grown in honesty and sincerity.

Vic's insecurity and dishonesty had threatened the whole relationship, but his profound attachment to Lynn gave him the spur to change. Counselling gave him the secure base from which to do it. The changes in Vic—with his willingness not to live in a romantic but false cloud-cuckoo land, his facing up to reality, the struggles he subsequently had with Lynn before she could accept this different person, and then his desire to find out who he was spiritually—show a man who is highly motivated to save his marriage, and someone who has a remarkable amount of what is called 'developmental mobility'. Often it will take only a tiny shift in either partner to save the whole relationship and to move it on. Vic showed he was capable of changing a great deal.

Not everyone, however, has the impetus to change, let alone be aware of their own needs and wants. This book is not a naïve celebration of the joys of marriage, but an exploration of the reality of life together, with all its bad moments, difficulties, conflicts, egocentricity and despair, as well as its positive qualities for change. It is intended to give couples hope in the midst of pain, to relieve them of some of the anxiety that besets them about being together, and provide an agenda for working out their problems. It holds out a long-term perspective: relationships do not just happen, but take a lifetime of commitment and effort together.

PART 1

The State of the Union

CHAPTER 1

Marriage: Dream and Reality

MARRIAGE, COHABITATION AND DIVORCE TODAY

'Divorces hit record high'; 'Breakdown rate is highest in Europe' screamed the British headlines early in 1995.

During the last months of 1994 and the first part of 1995, as this book was being researched and written, the news bulletins and papers were full not just of the seemingly endless line of government ministers resigning because of their marital misdemeanours, but of public figures and their multiple marriages. The deputy governor of the Bank of England, Rupert Pennant-Rea, quit his job because a scorned mistress had pulled the plug on their affair (a colleague said, 'On his third wife at forty-five, he was suspect from the start. Anyone can make a mistake, but this woman would have been his fourth wife'). A Church of England vicar, the Rev. Kit Chalcraft, was obliged by his bishop to leave his living of ten parishes because, twice divorced, his desire to marry a third time did not 'bear witness effectively to Christian standards of marriage'. In one week alone, celebrity couples ranging from Michael Jackson and Lisa-Marie Presley (together six months) and Richard Gere and Cindy Crawford (who managed three years) to Roger and Luisa Moore (married twenty-six years) and former Australian prime minister Bob Hawke and his wife Hazel (married thirty-eight years) were all reported to be separating. And in November 1995 the nation held its breath for the Princess of Wales' account of marital misery and adultery.

And yet both Messrs Pennant-Rea and Chalcraft, when embarking on their first venture in matrimony, doubtless believed wholeheartedly that they would remain in wedlock with the particular women they married till death did them part. The Moores, who had made it past their silver wedding anniversary, and the Hawkes, who had been together a lifetime, presumably entered marriage with the intention that it would be for ever.

It seems that the dream of an eternity of togetherness is fading. A report by the Joseph Rowntree Foundation says that annual marriage rates have fallen to their lowest levels since records began more than 150 years ago.[2] At the same time, divorce rates have climbed to a new peak. The 1993 *Population Trends* by the Office of Population Censuses and Surveys, published in 1995, reveals:

♥ there were 182,000 first-time marriages—about half the post-war peak of 340,000;

♥ the total number of marriages (including second and subsequent ones) was 299,000 compared with 426,000 in 1972;

♥ couples cohabit for longer before marrying;

♥ 90 per cent of divorced people cohabit before remarriage;

♥ more than one in five men and women were cohabiting in 1993 compared with one in seven in the mid-1980s;

and at the same time

♥ more than 160,000 couples divorced in 1992;

♥ an increase of 1,540 over the previous year;

♥ the highest number ever recorded in one year;

♥ marriages were dissolved after just 9.9 years on average.

Before we interpret this as the end of marriage as we know it we should perhaps look at history. Up till the first part of this century death brought as many marriages to an untimely end as divorce does today.

Our longevity now implies that a man and woman marrying in their twenties at the end of this century could have more than sixty years of conjugal life. Maybe this in part explains the phenomenon of the sizeable minority of couples who have begun to work out ways of living together which do not include formalized 'marriage'.

The paradox

The paradox is that most of us still get married. According to the 1993 figures, 58 per cent of Britons—nearly six out of ten adults—are currently married. It might be added that it is somewhat easier to get a marriage licence than a driving licence: no lessons are deemed necessary and no test of suitability is applied. We all think we are capable of making a go of it. 'All you need is love', we believe. But marriages are just as likely to crash as cars if we do not have the basic skills.

The reason is, perhaps, that marriage itself does not always deliver what it appears to offer. Its promise of security, companionship and fulfilment can turn into disappointment, loneliness and let-down. We may believe that in marrying we are taking a step away from our family of origin and into a grown-up relationship, yet in marriage we can replay familiar emotional and domestic scenarios, often acting the screaming and insecure baby rather than the mature adult we believe ourselves to be. Capable of high-level decision-taking at work, we may lapse into the frankly infantile at home.

And yet—and this is the paradox—despite the evidence of much divorce and more disappointment, the facts point to an apparently ineradicable optimism:

- more couples still stay together than separate

- many want to have a second (or third) go, demonstrating what Boswell reported Dr Johnson to have called a second marriage, 'the triumph of hope over experience'

- some even remarry the same person after a period apart;
- increasing numbers who cohabit model their relationships on traditional marriage.

This suggests that marriage still seems to be widely perceived as offering something desirable, as being a way of life which is potentially fulfilling and enhancing. 'Family life' now figures on the political agenda as a remedy for many of society's ills—from vandalism, theft and rape through football hooliganism to mental and physical illness. Politicians, despite their own peccadilloes, now seem to have grasped the fact that a durable and happy home life (subtext: 'marriage') gives children a better start in life. In the summer of 1994, Tony Blair, leader of the Labour Party, said:

It is best for kids to be brought up in a stable environment with two parents.

Conservative MP Alistair Burt (then Minister at the Department of Social Security) was not to be outdone:

If we are looking for stability, then I believe we are looking at lifelong commitment and marriage for preference, as statistics suggest that married relationships are more stable, more likely to endure and more likely to provide... warmth and security.

In this preliminary chapter we look at what marriage is, at what it offers which gives rise to this enduring optimism and makes it still so popular, at why couples marry and what they hope and expect of their marriage, and at why there is often such a painful gap between dream and reality.

What is marriage?

Marriage is changing. It is becoming increasingly hard to define what distinguishes it from cohabitation, except perhaps for those with a strong religious faith or background. The days when a marriage contract was arranged between a man and a woman to fulfil the obligations of kinship and society, to safeguard property or inheritance, are past. Gone, too, except in some of the more conservative corners of the Catholic Church, is the idea that the primary purpose of marriage is procreation. Also on the way out, since World War II, are rigid, gender-oriented roles within marriage, with *him* as provider and *her* as homemaker.

Explanations about what marriage is can be too simplistic, for the many factors affecting marriage today operate synergistically—their combined effect is greater than the sum of their separate effects. Nevertheless, it is possible to say that until the 'You've never had it so good' years of the late 1950s, 1960s and early 1970s, before inflation took hold, most married couples were more taken up with providing and maintaining a roof over their heads, enough to eat and clothes for themselves and their children. The humanist psychologist, Abraham Maslow, evolved a hierarchy of human needs, maintaining that the 'higher' needs (emotional, intellectual and spiritual) cannot be fulfilled until the more basic physical ones are securely met. In the past, therefore, when life was perhaps tougher materially, marriage was less oriented towards personal fulfilment and more towards social and financial objectives. Life expectancy was far shorter, and so sexual activity was more geared to reproduction.

In the 1960s women began to gain control over their fertility, there was fuller employment, and inflation and recession were only clouds on a distant horizon, invisible to most. With this relative security, men and women could attend more to issues of their personal development and fulfilment. Perhaps, now that the 'feel good' factor is evaporating and the disappearance of the permanently employed middle classes seems possible, marriage will again be seen as providing some sort of social and financial security, and the more profoundly emotional needs may take second place once more.

The Anglican *Book of Common Prayer* (1661) gives three reasons for marriage, rather than a definition of it, with the relationship between man and wife at the bottom of the list:

♥ the procreation of children

♥ a remedy against sin, and to avoid fornication

♥ 'for the mutual society, help, and comfort, that the one
  ought to have of the other'.

Nowadays the emphasis is far more on the third reason, the
relationship itself, and this is reflected in the Church of
England's Alternative Service Book (1980); here, sexual love is
described as having a symbolic place in the union, rather than
being solely for making babies, which process is now given a
secondary importance. Marriage has developed, so that now a
couple may

*... comfort and help each other, living faithfully together...
that with delight and tenderness they may know each other
in love, and, through the joy of their bodily union, may
strengthen the union of their hearts and lives.*

The revaluing of sex as something which both cements and
symbolizes the union is significant, for it is rare these days for
couples not to have full sexual intimacy before the wedding day
(only three of the sixty-five brides interviewed by Penny
Mansfield and Jean Collard in their portrait of new marriages,
The Beginning of the Rest of Your Life?, published in 1988,[3] were
virgins on their wedding night). The days have long
disappeared when it could be said that, as Dr John Marshall
wrote in the 1960s in his book, *Preparing for Marriage*,
'intercourse is, in fact, the unique thing which distinguishes the
marriage relationship from all others'.

If sexual love is in some way a symbol of the union of the
partners, it now appears the norm that this physical commitment takes place before any formal ceremony. The Roman
Catholic Church recognizes that it is the mutual commitment,
not the service, that forms the bond between man and wife. The
ministrations of the priest, and the presence of witnesses
representing the wider community, give marriage its public
dimension.

The testimony of 28-year-old William (quoted in the *Independent on Sunday*, 21 November 1993), who decided to marry after years of cohabiting, bears witness to the fact that the ritual of a wedding is a way of proclaiming what already is:

> *I don't want to change how we are, or what our relationship is, or how we've lived together—it's living together that's made me want to get married. But now I want us to marry with the maximum ritual, pomp and ceremony. You want to make it the most awe-inspiring and overwhelming event you can, with all the weight of history and tradition and a sense of cosmic significance. It's probably the most important thing you'll ever do, except giving birth or dying maybe.*

However, according to Mansfield and Collard, for many people premarital sexual activity was more a means of ensuring compatibility:

> *... it became clear that they* [some of the wives] *were trying to present the sexual relationship as having developed out of explicit commitment rather than as having pre-dated the commitment (the latter appeared to have been the actual case)... Sexual intimacy before marriage was particularly valued by the couples because they believed it allowed them to test their sexual compatibility. In their view, compatibility was a static component; you either were or were not compatible and it was important to discover this before marriage if possible.*

Cohabitation and marriage

As the twenty-first century dawns, it is valid to ask what exactly does define and differentiate the marriage relationship, given that so many couples now cohabit in unions which seem all but indistinguishable from marriage, as the old joke has it: 'Mary and Joseph weren't married but they had a stable relationship.'

One minister, Rev. Martin Dudley, reported this exchange with a young mother who was living with the father of her child:

*Without benefit of scholarship but with considerable
perception the mother pointed out that the public
commitment made by living together, the recognition and
support of their families, and the very fact of having a
thoroughly welcome baby amounted to marriage. They
would still have a marriage ceremony—when they could
afford it—in a year or two's time, and that would be a
celebration for their friends and families of that
commitment.*

Research shows that 58 per cent of couples who do marry have
lived together first and that in the case of remarriage after
divorce the percentage goes up to 90 per cent. For most
couples it is still a form of 'trial marriage'. The increase in
cohabitation over the past three or four decades is attributed to
a range of causes:

♥ a decline in religious practice and an increased
   acceptance of premarital sex;

♥ the effects of economic recession (and fear of its
   recurrence), which make both weddings and private
   housing less affordable;

♥ male unemployment: men may hesitate to marry if they
   cannot take on the traditional role of breadwinner;

♥ female employment: in maintaining their careers,
   women may wish to be financially independent.

One strong reason for *not* marrying, according to many young
people, is a desire to reject the influence of the parents'
marriage and to do something better—which perforce means
doing something different:

Stephen: *My boys have some very strong views about the
partnerships of their friends' parents, and that gives them
the framework. I don't think they would assume harmony
is the norm. They've seen too many of their friends' parents
where harmony is far from the norm.*

The wheel of the past two and a half centuries has come round nearly full circle, for it is only since 1753 that English law has refused to grant legal status to open and stable cohabitation. The legality of 'common law' marriages still obtains in Scotland, and in France and elsewhere 'concubinage' is legally recognized. An article by Clifford Longley in the *Daily Telegraph,* 15 February 1995 points out that the phrase 'living in sin'

> *was largely invented by eighteenth-century clergy to shame their parishioners towards church marriage. And there was a substantial marriage fee to be collected, a useful boost to clergy incomes. Once people realize this history, it may make cohabiting couples that little bit easier for the Church to live with.*

A report, *Something to Celebrate,* issued in the summer of 1995 by the Church of England, said that in some cases what they coyly call these 'non-ceremonial marriages' are indeed marriages in all but name. The Archbishop of Canterbury then weighed in to support the ideal of lifelong marriage. Earlier in 1995 the then Archbishop of York, Dr John Habgood, had made a plea to the government to increase tax incentives in order to persuade couples out of their 'sin' and into the presumably holier estate of matrimony. However, it is doubtful that stable, committed partners would be lured to the altar or registry office for the sake of a few hundred pounds, as is shown by this interview, from a *Daily Telegraph* article of the same date by Elizabeth Grice:

> *Marriage could not offer us any more than we already have so, although it would please both sets of parents, it would make no difference to us. I certainly wouldn't get married if someone paid me. The broken marriages of our friends and our parents' generation have made us wary— not of marriage itself but of jumping into it.*

Many who choose to marry after a long period of cohabitation often do so for expediency rather than any desire to change the nature of their relationship, as these author interviews show. One couple married after nineteen years together:

Wife: He had asked me before, but he asked again just before we left Australia because he thought that travelling round the world we would have to face prejudice of one sort or another... it would make it more difficult not being married—with immigration.

Five years on the husband said:

It has made no difference at all; it was irrelevant except perhaps in other people's attitudes, especially Yvonne's parents.

Often, couples will marry when the woman becomes pregnant. Sometimes, however, they wait until their children are older. Here is one husband whose reason for marrying was to spare his daughter difficulty or embarrassment at a new school:

It didn't make no [sic] difference to me. We went to the registry office and I was back working on the market in half an hour. We'd been together eight years or so. Sasha was going to school then and we wanted to give her an identity.

But older couples often appear to be more bound by convention. Here a couple (he in his early fifties, she aged forty) speak about their cohabitation, which started not long after both had been divorced, as a prelude to an inevitable marriage:

Wife: For me there wasn't any alternative. It was the way I was. I would not have entered into a full-time and permanent relationship without getting married. It was just the way I am.

Husband: It was cohabitation with the intention of getting married.

Wife: I don't think it occurred to us that it would be anything else. It seemed to have occurred to everybody else that it would be, but it didn't occur to us.

But for the majority of those interviewed who had experienced both long-term cohabitation and marriage, there appeared to be little difference between a union which had been solemnized and one which had not, though some of the wives reported that they felt more secure.

'Security' is, in fact, one of the major, if illusory, distinctions between marriage and living together. William, quoted above in the *Independent on Sunday*, said:

> *I was away on a trip, and I read an Ian McEwan book in which two people get married. There's some phrase like 'enjoying the certainty of their future happiness together'. I thought: 'Yes—that's the point, we have to get married.' If you're not married you don't have that certainty, and there always lurks some dark possibility that you will at some point separate. So you can be deliriously happy from day to day, but you don't have that hand on the future.*

Alas for William and those who think like him, recent research suggests that couples in the UK who have lived together before marriage have higher rates of divorce than those who have not done so. Research in 1992 showed that couples who married in the 1980s after having cohabited had a 50 per cent greater chance of divorcing within five years of marriage than couples who had not.[4] When the marriage had lasted as long as eight years the likelihood of divorce went up to 60 per cent more than those who had no experience of living together. These findings are echoed by those in Sweden, the Netherlands, other European countries and Canada.

The reasons for this may be more circumstantial than causal, as outlined in a document from One Plus One, the marriage and partnership research charity. Studies of current cohabitees show they are less religious and have a more liberal attitude to divorce than currently married couples, which may perhaps suggest that for them marriage is less of a permanent commitment. Premarital cohabitation is also connected with a range of other behaviours and views which are associated with a greater likelihood of divorce. These include:

- ♥ marrying at a registry office rather than in a church;

- ♥ divorce in the families of origin;

- ♥ living in an urban rather than a rural setting;

- ♥ holding less stereotypical views on the roles of men and women.

Thus the connection between cohabitation and subsequent divorce may spring from similar factors being at play in both, rather than being cause and effect.

But this still does not define any distinction—other than one of possible longevity—between marriage and a union which is not legally formalized. In many cases, unless we take the Christian stance that marriage symbolically and sacramentally reflects the relationship between Christ and his Church, there can be little difference except in fiscal and legal matters. For most people today the theology will make little sense, and so we have to interpret the difference in other language.

A public statement of intent?

A central point in the distinction between marriage and cohabitation is the willingness of the man and woman to make a lifelong and *public* commitment to each other *and to the relationship*, with the expectation that this commitment will hold good throughout the course of their life together, supporting and protecting both the individuals *and* the partnership and any children they may have. Marriage somehow implies that the couple have both a place and a stake in society, and that the unit they are creating together out of two existing units is, while intensely personal and private, also part of the fabric of the wider community, so that the couple belong both to each other and to the outside world. This evolution, from being a couple with eyes only for each other to being a partnership which is integrated into the social environment, constitutes a large part of the process which is marriage. The stages of marriage, which form the subject of the main part of this book, show how this happens in practice. The Western world, with its Christian influence, is not the only one where the prevailing culture invests marriage with this social dimension: a Buddhist, for example, defined marriage as two people of the opposite sex living in harmony for the procreation of children *and for the general good of humanity*.

By marrying, then, a couple make a public statement about their relationship, which in turn is recognized as part of society. The marriage may not necessarily endure longer than the period of cohabitation, but the couple have declared their intention to the world that their marriage should be a lifelong investment; in theory at least, the community returns its support. It is doubtful whether mere financial help for married couples (in the form of tax allowances—with less, consequently, for single parents) would constitute sufficient social buttressing of the institution to persuade cohabitees to the altar.

A journey together?

'persevering endeavour... a complete and intimate life-partnership and association'[5]

The second aspect of this lifelong commitment is that it implies and demands a constant and ongoing process of renewal and review, and that this process has a validity in its own right. As a married couple the man and the woman are building something together, and this edifice will never be fully finished or complete. Rather like painting the famous railway bridge over the river Forth in Scotland, there will always be parts which must be repaired, renovated, redone and gone over again. Marriage is the process of becoming a couple. To use another simile, it is like a pilgrimage in which the journey is as important as the destination—the means is an end in itself.

Some definitions[6] suggest that a marriage can somehow defined by certain characteristics, not shared by other relationships:

The married vocation calls for a radical and freely given commitment from each to the other. It demands fidelity and self-sacrifice. It is meant to be lifelong and exclusive.

*These are not externally imposed requirements, but **the innate characteristics of married love** [my emphasis].*

Many cohabitees will protest that fidelity, sacrifice, exclusivity and longevity are also present in their relationships. However, the testimony of Keith, a divorced man of fifty-three interviewed by the *Independent on Sunday*, November 1993, suggests that his marriage was somehow defined both retrospectively and negatively by the agony he experienced in its dissolution, and that this sprang partly from the *public* nature of marriage:

I've had relationships that lasted longer and were more serious than my marriage. Breaking off any of them has never involved the pain of my divorce. You've stood in front of your family and your maker and thought it was for life. You've gone through that ritual and made that commitment. And the bubble bursts. There's a bigger sense of failure.

For better, for worse?

However, it would be rather negative to say 'that was a marriage' only when we can look back and see that it lasted till death and that husband and wife were faithful to each other. The following account by a marriage counsellor suggests there is more to marriage:

I am supporting a friend whose husband is having an affair. I think one of the most difficult things she is finding is the pressure of 'friends' to dump her husband. They suggest she is compromising herself by letting him still live with her. They suggest she is degrading herself, etc. In her weaker moments she begins to wonder if she is wrong to keep trying to save the marriage. When she is strong from praying and 'being' herself, she knows that as long as she keeps the communication channels open there is still hope. She can't be letting herself down by still loving him. She is loving the man she married whilst recognizing his difficulties at the current time. It takes a lot of strength! But the conflict is in the real world where self-preservation often overrules caring for others.

It could be said that the process of 'becoming', mentioned above, could apply equally to the committed couple relationship which is not as formalized as marriage, but which in all other ways is identical. But it is perhaps the combination of the private process with the public nature of the legalized union that distinguishes marriage from cohabitation. The public part needs public support, and not only in the form of tax incentives. The Law Commission, in its *Report on the Grounds for Divorce* (November 1990), pointed out that:

> *There is sound public interest in helping preserve those marriages which can be saved.*

The distinction between the private and public relationship, however, has narrowed significantly over the course of the twentieth century, especially during the last four decades. The quality of the relationship itself has gained primacy over the framework or structure of the way of life (domestic, financial and familial) that marriage offers couples. The institution has given way to the relationship, the 'togetherness' of which Mansfield and Collard's young couples often spoke. What has emerged is called by sociologists the 'companionate' marriage, a search for personal, emotional and sexual fulfilment.

An unconscious quest?

This fulfilment can come about only as the result of our personal growth. This is one of the paradoxes of marriage: to develop as individuals and to learn to become independent beings we have to be in relationship. We cannot learn about ourselves if we not involved with other people, and conversely our relationships will not be fulfilling if we have not attained a degree of self-awareness. We yearn for closeness, yet can fear the very thing we desire so much. The marital therapist Robin Skynner says in his book, *One Flesh: Separate Persons*:

> *Marriage is always an attempt at growth, at healing oneself and finding oneself again, however disastrously any particular attempt may fail for lack of sufficient understanding or external help.*

Some of those who write on marriage, notably Dr Jack Dominian, have heavily emphasized this healing aspect of marriage.

From time to time those who are either voluntarily or involuntarily single protest at these exclusive claims. It is worth noting that any loving and close relationship can, to a certain extent, bring about self-knowledge and promote growth. What Jean Vanier, the founder of the l'Arche communities for people with disabilities, writes (in *Man and Woman He Made Them*) of these communities is as true for marriage as it is for any relationship:

> *Many of those... have suffered... They have been neither accepted nor loved; in their fragility and anguish they can neither accept nor love themselves... This time of healing is often long... In discovering the need for others, who also have their joys, pains, needs, the person is able to live and share with them a covenant relationship. An ability to join the 'body', which is community, implies that the person is willing to make the transition from 'the others for me' to 'me for the others'. The decision to love and to take on responsibility is a fundamental choice...* [which] *must be accompanied by continuing efforts to grow beyond selfishness and the world of darkness and fear, which is in each one of us.*

Why marry?

Those embarking on a path which they hope will bring fulfilment will do so with high expectations, despite—or perhaps because of—the evidence of their own families of origin or those of their friends.

Expectations

Where expectations run high there is a greater risk that disappointment will follow not far behind. When partners fail to live up to the impossibility of each other's desires, to the dreams and longings which they project both knowingly and unawares onto the other, then the resultant hurt, anger and bitterness go a long way towards explaining the paradox of statistics which tell us that most of us marry, yet divorce happens more frequently than ever before:

Where there are false or unrealistic expectations of love, coupled with many examples of marriages ending rather than persevering when the going gets tough, it is little wonder that many find it difficult to sustain their mutual commitment.

Cardinal Basil Hume

When asked the question 'Why marry?', the following are some random answers which give differing reasons for matrimony and people's expectations of it:

- love; attraction
- companionship
- remedy to loneliness
- sex
- to fulfil expectations of parents
- common interests
- panic at being on the shelf
- cowardice; couldn't say 'no'
- pregnancy
- expectations of happiness; fantasy
- to have children
- to get away from something (family, job, country)
- for status
- for mutual support
- on the rebound

These suggest that our expectations of the relationship are at three levels:

♥ social (class, money, religion, and so forth)

♥ conscious personal issues (for instance, physical and intellectual stimulus, feeling at home with someone, common interests)

♥ unconscious factors (being 'in love', 'chemistry', and so on).

These, as we shall see in the next chapter, correlate to the three 'levels' at which we select our mate.

In the Mansfield and Collard book, based on interviews with young couples during the earliest months of their marriages, the newly-weds talked of their hopes and expectations, which reflect these different 'levels':

The usual things—a nice home and sooner or later a family—and I'd like our life together to be the most important thing rather than his job.

A good marriage to somebody I can trust, to be fairly well off, have children and love each other.

I want to have our own house, have three kids, have a good life together, share the responsibilities with the children—and retire to the seaside.

Mansfield and Collard go on to summarize what those entering matrimony expect of their life together:

With marriage comes [sic] a home of one's own, a home life, respect as a married person, and, above all else, security, since it offers a framework for the future. Of course most of these goals could have been achieved in other ways, although never so conveniently in one action. Marriage also has an added bonus—a partner with whom to create and share this new life. The marital relationship provides someone to share a home life with, a regular sexual partner, a confidante, someone who is 'on your side' and who cares for you and about you.

But they don't come easily. As G.A. Studdert-Kennedy pointed out in 1928 in *The Warrior, the Woman and the Christ,*

The voluntary sacrifice of freedom is the paradox of love.

When we choose to marry we give up part of ourselves—a large proportion of our liberty and independence. In the early days of marriage we willingly merge our identities to create a new entity. The perception is that what we shall gain is greater than what we may lose. But it is not a once-and-for-all action, rather an ongoing process which must be constantly reviewed and renewed, demanding sometimes a Sisyphean heroism. Relationship, it has been said, is like elastic: it is strong at first, but grows slacker, and has to be renewed if things are not to fall down.

Sharing our existence with another person can be a joy; it is also hard work. It is a delicate and difficult process which requires sensitivity and tolerance. We are all needy people; we crave closeness but may also fear what it involves. We may not have the awareness to understand *our* needs, let alone those of our partner; neither may we have the language to express our deepest longings. The daily round challenges us to continual compromise, but if we are fragile we may sometimes feel we lose too much of ourselves by giving way, apologizing or attempting to communicate our feelings, when our natural reaction would be to shout or sulk. It is a cliché of local newspaper reporting of Golden and Diamond Weddings that an elderly couple will invariably say that 'give and take' is the recipe for long and contented years of marriage, but it is one which has much truth in it.

But whether we are capable of giving depends largely on where we are in our personal journey of development. In the next chapter, therefore, we explore how and why we choose our partner on this journey, and the effect that this may have on the journey itself.

Summary

Marriage has changed radically during this century, and the transition from an institution, which had social and economic benefits as well as personal ones, to a more egalitarian partnership, from which two individuals expect emotional and physical well-being and fulfilment, has accelerated since the last war. This new 'companionate' relationship requires social skills of communication, availability, affirmation and resolution of conflict which are not innate and must be learned. The evolution of marriage has narrowed the difference between the 'committed couple' relationship (cohabitation) and 'marriage', to the point where, in this secular age, the distinction is frequently blurred.

However, figures suggest that those marrying split up less frequently, or after a longer period, than those cohabiting, so there is some element of endurance and security which still attaches to matrimony. The public solemnization, the vows and promises exchanged, add up to something more than a commitment to live together, and this appears in some way to spring from the public or social dimension of marriage.

Marriage is still popular, even though divorce figures have risen rapidly, and 'family life' and its supposedly traditional values figure on the political and ecclesiastical agendas as being a panacea for social evils. Young couples are attracted to marriage because it appears to promise a passage into full adulthood, stability, security, a new way of life, usually a place to live away from parental constraints, with sex on tap, and the creation of something new and unique—a couple. People who have been married before usually want to remarry. The expectations of married life, which are material, physical and emotional, are high nowadays, and disillusion and disappointment can quickly follow.

The consensus of opinion is that 'happy' marriages are founded, and thrive, on an awareness of our own needs along with a sensitivity to those of our partner; on the ability and willingness to communicate effectively; on some sacrifice of self; and on compromise and trust—all within the safe container of a relationship to whose continuance both partners are committed. However, for many reasons one or both partners may be incapable of these qualities.

CHAPTER 2

The Marriage of True Minds?

WHY AND HOW WE CHOOSE OUR MATE

Why and how do we manage to end up with our partner? Was there really just that one person for us, earmarked by fate and predestined through eternity to share our bed, the trips to the supermarket, the dirty nappies and eventually the pension? Could we have married anyone else? Would it have been better—or worse? Will the decision we made at twenty-four still hold good at forty-four? Will we still be needed at sixty-four? And, since we live longer these days, how will we feel at eighty-four?

Laura and Henry

Laura was twenty-eight and had been married for six years to Henry, nineteen years her senior, and they had three children. Laura came for counselling as she could no longer cope with Henry's 'laziness' and 'fecklessness'. Laura's father had died when she was ten and bordering on puberty. At eighteen she had been deeply attracted to Henry in what was her first significant relationship, drawn to his protectiveness and what seemed to her to be his maturity. Henry, however, had no steady job, although he was a graduate and a qualified teacher, and he did not exert himself to find one. Gradually, Laura found herself in the position of breadwinner, taking control of finances and decisions, and shouldering most of the responsibility for both the household and the children. Laura's brother had pointed out what he saw as Henry's immaturity and irresponsibility before the couple married, but Laura had gone ahead. Laura now found it increasingly impossible to cope with a job, her three small children, and Henry—whom she now found as difficult and demanding as a child.

We shall return to Laura and Henry at the end of this chapter.

As we lay entwined in each other's arms after a romantic candlelit dinner, I gazed at the man I was going to marry and asked myself how I could once have considered him the worst blind date in my life.[7]

I saw this person come into the room... and it was perfectly obvious to me that this was the person I was going to marry. He more or less came straight over to where I was. Nothing attracted him to me initially, nothing at all. But for a long time I knew I'd marry him, though it didn't seem a very sensible choice [wife in research interview].

These two very different reminiscences demonstrate how complex it is to try to define what attracts us to the person we eventually marry. The first shows that the magnet pulling the couple together was stronger than the initial mutual dislike and apparent incompatibility. The second shows that immediate attraction can be deep and powerful, and can override the evidence of our eyes and the reasoning of our brain.

So what are the qualities that affect our choices? This chapter is a brief analysis of some of the 'how and why' involved in choosing our life partner, and it also addresses how these factors affect whether they will still need us, let alone feed us, when we're sixty-four.

Across a crowded room...

Research interviews with couples included the question, 'What initially attracted you to your partner?' Answers ranged from the practical:

- I thought he'd make a good father

to the cerebral and cultural:

- she had her thinking cap on
- we were compatible culturally
- she had a broad range of interests

through the admiring:

- he was a strong personality. He seemed to have got it all together and knew where he was going
- he was just a warm person

and the indifferent:

- when I went into this room for this dance and three girls came in, and Pattie was the best of the bunch. That was the initial thing, and because she was happy to go out with me the next day it just grew from that. And she's a nice person

and the curious:

- he didn't take his eyes off me for weeks

to the downright lustful:

- she leant forward to get some toast and I saw her right tit and was mesmerized.

These were the initial impressions of ordinary people who met by chance in ordinary places—at a party, in a lift, in a church hall, on a course, in a student residence—and made a fleeting but significant assessment 'across a crowded room'. They give us our first clue about the process of mate selection: this preliminary 'triage' is not usually entirely random, because as often as not the proverbial room is crowded with people who have similar backgrounds, professions, qualifications or interests. A man and a woman on, say, an intensive language course for business people will immediately have something in common; a couple who first glimpse each other in church are likely to share a similar system of beliefs and values; those who meet in the office, or ten-pin bowling, or on a skiing holiday have at once a point of contact, however superficial.

The reasons that got us into the same 'crowded room' (or wherever) and initiated the contact suggest there is often a broad similarity in social and cultural backgrounds, a reasonable match of intelligence and the likelihood of some shared value systems. In the majority of cases, these will form the first step on the road to the registry office or altar.

Looks aren't everything

In our fantasies, good looks may have more importance than they do in reality. Men in particular tend to describe stereotypes when they try to define what they find attractive in a woman, and these 'identikit' pictures often seem to be heavily coloured by celluloid and newsprint images. 'The blonde' has enduring appeal—tall, slim but with large breasts. One man who described his ideal as the stereotypical 'tall leggy blonde' had actually been in love for some years with a rather heavily-built woman with short legs and dark hair. For women, physical attributes seem to be ultimately less important and they tend to let go of fantasies earlier. However, ideas about beauty probably count less than the reality for both sexes, for we are strongly influenced by other, less conscious, factors, one of which can be an unrecognized resemblance to a significant figure in our past. This can result in a marked physical resemblance between husband and wife:

We've been told we could be taken for brother and sister. In fact, apparently I look very like Robert's mother. His father says I'm like her in personality as well.

Robert's mother had died the year before he met Pattie.

In practice the initial lure is rarely purely physical, though it can exercise a powerful pull—as in the case of the man quoted above who glimpsed his future partner's right breast when she bent over a table. But just as often the opposite is true, and both

43

men and women report not just a lack of physical attraction, but something bordering on revulsion:

- I thought he was a bit of a wimp to begin with, and his trousers were too short.

- Ugh! She was wearing a fur coat—and smoking!

- I thought 'What a creep!'

- To begin with, his look was all wrong—short, balding, stocky... not exactly Prince Charming. More like the Frog Prince.[8]

- Beth was attractive, all right, but when I introduced myself, she shook my hand limply, without smiling, and didn't look me in the eye. Already, about fifteen seconds into the date, I knew she didn't like me.[9]

- Look at two 'heart-throbs' who are currently held up to us as male aesthetic ideals—Richard Gere and Hugh Grant. The first has a face like a battered potato; the second, egg-like lilac eyes and an effeminate quality that may appeal to some men, but not to a red-blooded woman.[10]

But something more complex is happening when we become attracted to someone, and it happens unknown to us. There are less conscious reasons why these first contacts evolve into significant relationships.

The heart has its reasons which reason knows nothing of.
Blaise Pascal

These are the unconscious forces which are the result of our early years, of what has happened or not happened to us, and—importantly—how our family of origin acts and interacts. Both our relationship with our parents and the model of relationship provided by them are more significant than we usually realize, and many factors springing from these will drive us towards one person or another, and channel us, despite ourselves, into certain patterns of behaviour, ways of interacting, and even methods of solving problems and making decisions.

An exercise devised by family therapists in the United States provides a strong clue to what is actually going on when we mark out someone across that proverbial crowded room. In the Family Systems Exercise a group of people, previously unknown to one another, are put into a room together and each person is asked to select someone else from the group who may in some way resemble a member of their family of origin, or who seems likely to be able to fulfil a role in that family which had been missing. When they have talked a while about the reasons for selecting whom they did, and discussed family background, each pair is then asked to choose another pair, and get together in a foursome as a 'family' and negotiate who plays what role in the family. What guided the participants to make these choices gradually emerges, and amazing similarities in the family systems of behaviour and interaction almost always become apparent.

What seem like bizarre coincidences can happen in any gathering where strangers meet. Joanna, a woman in her early forties, was at a conference in a part of the country she had never been before. After arrival and registration, delegates were asked to pair off with someone and talk for fifteen minutes. No guidance was given about how to select the other person. Joanna went over to a younger woman called Jean, who in fact had simultaneously selected her. The two women had ostensibly little in common—they were different in age, education, background, and lived far distant from each other—but what was disclosed in further discussion was that both had been deeply emotionally involved with the same man. They subsequently discovered many other strange 'coincidences'. It was not until some years later, when analyzing what had drawn her to Jean across the room, that Joanna realized that Jean had carrotty red hair, pale skin and freckles similar to those of her own mother.

One of the conclusions from the Family Systems Exercise was that two individuals from families that have similar patterns, or 'systems', will often be strongly drawn to each other, however dissimilar the pair may appear on the surface and however much they may rationalize their choice on the grounds of shared interests—or, in the case of a male-female encounter, sexy looks.

Even when it appears that 'opposites attract', there exist potent underlying factors of resemblance. People home in on others whom they unconsciously perceive may be able to fill a lack in early significant, usually parental, relationships. This unconscious process, known in psychospeak as 'transference' (the displacement of attributes belonging to a figure in our past onto someone with whom we are currently in relationship) will dictate our feelings and reactions to the person. When it happens, it can make the other person seem enormously attractive. We will engage with them because our 'wise unconscious' glimpses the chance of reworking a past relationship which failed us in some way; in other words, we may resolve a conflict and heal a wound.

'Slave to two lovers'

This may explain why the divorced and widowed often seem to end up, if they remarry, with someone who in many ways is a replica of the first partner. Neither is this confined to married relationships: Gerald Kaufman's review of Barbara Leaming's biography of Katharine Hepburn in *The Times*, 25 March 1995, bore the heading 'Slave to two lovers':

> *To become infatuated with one drunken scoundrel may be regarded as a misfortune. To be hopelessly in love with two such reprobates looks like masochism... For more than a quarter of a century Katharine Hepburn was involved, concurrently, in liaisons with the film director, John Ford, and the actor, Spencer Tracy. Both were married. Both strung her along with intimations that they would leave their wives to marry her. Both let her down. Both were disgusting, falling-down alcoholics. Her addiction to both caused Hepburn to sacrifice giving birth to the child for which she longed.*

This sort of repetition of painful scenarios can happen as much in the provincial English towns of Harpenden or Hull as it does in Hollywood, both outside and within the legal relationship of marriage. A mistress or a lover can be uncannily like the partner at home. The following is an extract from an article by Libby Purves in *The Times* , 20 January 1995, about Ken Dunn, whose dead body was fought over by wife and mistress:

... Mr Dunn is revealed as a familiar type: not a serial monogamist but a photocopy polygamist. He led not a double life but a twin one. For twenty years he lived partly with his wife—greying curly hair, with big square spectacles—and partly with his mistress, Ms Cooper: greying curly hair, two years older, more big square specs. The women acknowledged one another with guarded tolerance: they had a lot in common. On weekdays Mr Dunn lived at Ms Cooper's; at weekends with his wife. The houses are similar... Both homes had dogs called Kim... Such unadventurous adventurers are all around. Certain men have an uncanny knack of pairing off with the same woman over and over again in different editions... the older man who disentangles himself from an unhappy marriage and immediately takes up with a clone of his wife: another commanding redhead, another giggly clinger, another intense neurotic.

The unconscious psychological factors which are at work when contacts between men and women take root and blossom into romance could be summed up in the rather pessimistic dictum, 'Needy people need needy people.' Although we are all needy in some way or another, the greater the lack in our lives the harder we fall in love—at no matter what age.

What happens across the crowded room, and subsequently, goes something like this: we all have aspects within our deepest emotions and personality that we reject and distance from ourselves, because we were made aware in our earliest years, if not months, that they were not acceptable in our family. These emotions and their manifestation seem shameful and painful to us, and we hide them away so they become our unconscious 'shadow' side.

Thus a family that has never learned to deal safely with anger and is frightened of its power will emit strong messages (verbal and non-verbal) to its members that anger is taboo. The child catches on to this pretty quickly and, in order to win love and acceptance, will dissociate from the emotion and hide it under an appearance which is quite opposite; the child may thus become an excessively calm, passive and phlegmatic personality. In another example, children whose families can't cope with sexual matters may grow up fearful of the powerful drive of their own sexuality, and may become frigid. We all, to a greater or lesser degree, grow up fearing that if certain parts of our needs and emotions were visible to the outside world we should be neither lovable nor acceptable to others, nor functional as human beings. Our unconscious exercises its own logic in trying to defend and protect us from the resulting pain of rejection. These areas, which we unknowingly hide, are the parts we consider unlovely and unlovable. It is here that we will find our 'shadow side'—the needy parts of ourselves, the scars and wounds we cover or disown, but whose healing is the quest we embark on in our significant adult relationships.

When we fall in love we unknowingly see the hidden, shadow part of ourselves mirrored in the other, with the effect that we have that euphoric exhilarating sensation of recognition, of discovering parts of ourselves we didn't know existed. We feel completed when we are with our beloved and that we belong to each other; we are transformed by being in love. We feel we are beautiful and lovable, and we perceive the other as wonderful. Each becomes a mirror for the other, which we hold up so we can see our own personality and behaviour reflected back at us—we 'project' ourselves onto the other. At this time we are more in love with ourselves than the other as they really are.

During this initial attraction, we emit unconscious messages geared to the fulfilment of our needs and the healing of our wounds. The signals are picked up by those who, because they are emitting similar messages, are unconsciously able to read and decode them. This results in a psychological recognition which is often rationalized (as attractive looks or personality) and which, when added to a not dissimilar background, culture and set of values, produces a couple who believe they were made for each other.

The wise unconscious

These unknown, shadow areas lie hidden in the unconscious depths of ourselves, lost to us till we find the soul-mate who may often have similar needs, fears, patterns of behaviour and wounds. Our lover awakes our dreams, hopes and longings, and emotional fulfilment at last seems within our grasp. At a conscious level it may seem that 'opposites attract', for the parts of ourselves which we have repressed are frequently the ones that are eminently visible in our partner's personality and behaviour, and the converse of the visible surface ones which characterize us to the outside world and which we have cultivated since our earliest days in order to be acceptable.

Those who have read Joanna Trollope's *The Rector's Wife* will remember the staid and repressed clergyman, Peter Bouverie, and his theatrical vivacious wife, Anna. The rector, who has been passed over for promotion after a lifetime of sacrifice and poverty, is completely unable to acknowledge the bitterness which has pervaded his life or to do what he most wants—to hit out angrily against an unjust God. He projects these unacceptable feelings which he cannot deal with onto his wife, telling everyone that she is harder hit and more disappointed than anyone. It is left to Anna to carry his anger, and in the end to do the breaking out and the rebelling against the church that he is unable to do.

Nicholas and Harriet

Nicholas, a businessman, had had a turbulent upbringing by an alcoholic mother who was given to violent, attention-seeking, dramatic acts. Nicholas learned early to suppress his emotions, and was considered by colleagues and friends as hard, cold, emotionless and a very private individual. He rigidly controlled himself—his eating and his drinking, and his environment—and was a physical fitness fanatic. He found both physical and emotional intimacy difficult (the former means letting go, the latter requires vulnerability). His holidays, however, always had an element of danger: mountaineering, pot-holing, white-water canoeing, for example. When he unexpectedly and unwillingly fell deeply in love, it was with Harriet who was widely considered to be a strong, powerful and professional woman. In fact, Harriet's independence masked a yearning to be supported, loved and cared for. As the relationship progressed she revealed more and more of this 'shadow' side; she became dependent on Nicholas, and there were dramatic scenes during which her fear of being abandoned became painfully evident.

Nicholas thus found himself replaying scenes from his childhood, with a weeping, childlike woman. The passions he witnessed in Harriet were the ones he so feared in himself: they were the ones that had scarred his early life and that until then he had successfully and rigidly kept at bay.

The controlled Nicholas and the seemingly strong, independent Harriet demonstrate that we can select our partner in an unconscious drive to deal with these difficult, painful and unacceptable areas which we have rejected and hidden away, and to have a 'second go' at resolving the difficulties and conflicts of our childhood. In this case it worked. Nicholas was able to give Harriet sufficient nurturing and proof of his love to convince her that he wasn't going to abandon her. At the same time, he helped her by giving her boundaries and showing that he was not going to tolerate tantrums and scenes. Harriet was able to put Nicholas in touch with the emotional and passionate part of himself, and give that back to him. Both grew emotionally.

Facing reality

At some point we must recognize clearly which characteristics 'belong' to us, and which belong to our beloved. This is what is happening when the rose-coloured spectacles of romance come off and we see our partner as they really are. Now is the time when somehow we have to reclaim our shadow side and integrate it back into ourselves in order to become a whole person. This is a difficult time in any relationship, for it is the part of our journey together which is the passage from being 'in love' to the beginnings of love. The purpose of this journey of love is to enable us to be the people we were created to be—our real selves.

The result, however, is not always wholeness and healing. Sometimes we strive to keep our unacceptable aspects safely away from ourselves and contained within our partner. If we cannot eventually recognize them and take them back, then our personalities will not grow and develop but stay for ever at the emotional stage at which they 'stuck' in childhood. Our early conflicts will be perpetuated and the knife turned in old wounds. Our adult relationships will then not be fully mature, even though in other spheres we may be able to function in the grown-up world. Sometimes, both husband and wife will unconsciously collude with each other in not taking back their projections, because in both families of origin that particular characteristic was not acceptable.

But if we do not take back or 'own' what belongs to us and to no one else, then old family patterns of behaviour will eventually re-emerge—dominance and submission, punishment and deprivation, aggression and depression, anger and retreat. We shall then play the same tune on the same record for ever, stuck in the same groove, and because it is so familiar we will find comfort and security in that. Moreover, unless we can change the record, our children and perhaps our children's children will dance to that tune as well. It gives new meaning to the awesome words of the Old Testament God to his people:

I punish a parent's fault in the children,
the grandchildren, and the great-grandchildren.
Exodus 20:5, Jerusalem Bible

Bernard and Sonia

Bernard was fifty-two and Sonia forty-three when they came for counselling. Bernard was from a South African family and was a successful surgeon; Sonia had a working-class background in south London and had been a nurse. Bernard was a powerful man, physically and emotionally; his mother had been undemonstrative, cold and lacking in affection. He lived in the sphere of the rational and the logical, and nobody ever worsted him in an argument. Sonia's family had been chaotic and noisily quarrelsome, and she had always been in the middle. There had been no romance between her and Bernard; he had never declared his love. Sonia had fallen initially for Bernard's family, which had seemed to her to get on without quarrelling, and she saw him as a saviour who would rescue her from continual rows. Now, twenty years on, Sonia yearned for touch, affection, sex, love—of which Bernard appeared incapable. Their youngest daughter suffered badly from asthma, which seemed linked to family tension, and Sonia found herself in the middle of rows between father and daughter.

The roots of Bernard's and Sonia's impasse seemed to lie clearly in their own families of origin, and their daughter's disease was probably a legacy of this as well. Through counselling, Sonia changed. She had spent many years blaming Bernard: 'You were never in love with me,' had been her reproach. But now she was able to speak of her own feelings, owning that these were hers. Bernard, however, remained stuck and immovable—where he was in his family situation of fifty years back—seeing no reason to change. It would take only a small shift, an acknowledgment of his feelings, to change the whole marital dynamic.

Two psychologists, Joseph Luft and Harry Ingham, created something they called the Johari Window (a conflation of their first names) to show how the shadow self can emerge within relationship (see facing page):

Snake or ladder?

We love inasmuch as love was present in the first great affair of our lives.' [11]

Our personality, forged in our earliest relationships and shaped by our family's pattern of behaviour and interaction, pushes us to make all kinds of choices of which we are largely unaware. It has been said that all our significant adult relationships are a series of transferences to some extent or another. For example, the woman who, when asked what first attracted her to her

THE JOHARI WINDOW[12]

A Arena: known to self and others
1. Free and open exchange of information
2. Behaviour is public and freely available
3. The arena increases in size as trust grows

B Blind spot: perceived by others, hidden from self
1. Self-awareness is lacking
2. Motives, feelings and behaviours perceived by others
3. Communicated by what is said and how
4. Communicated non-verbally

The internal boundaries of the window are movable: up, down, across, according to the willingness to disclose oneself and give and ask for feedback.

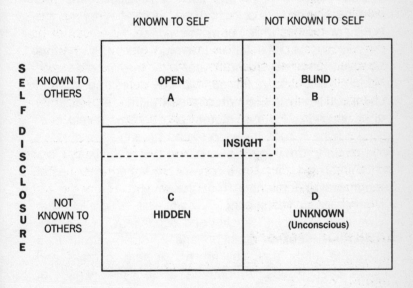

C Façade: hidden from others, known to self
1. Private and secret
2. Rarely disclosed
3. Fear of hurt, rejection, judgment

D Unknown: hidden from self and others
The realm of the unconscious and subconscious

future husband, replied, 'I thought he'd make a good father,' was undoubtedly yearning for him to be a father to *her*. If achieved in an atmosphere of love, nurture and trust, these unconscious regressions to earlier relationships can give us what we lacked, promote our healing and enable us to move on. They can be a ladder to personal growth.

Michael and Jackie

Michael's parents had been shopkeepers and rarely had time for their two sons, who spent their holidays at children's camps. There had been little physical demonstration of affection in the home. Michael was shy and uncertain, and had not been out with many girls when, at twenty-three, he met Jackie, who was nineteen. Jackie's father had been an alcoholic who had committed suicide and Jackie had had to look after her younger brothers and sisters while her mother worked.

Jackie and Michael fell in love and married two years later. Their first baby came a year after they married, and their second quickly followed. Michael dates the start of marital conflict from the birth of their children. At that time, Jackie ceased to be 'his' mother and became a real one; Michael (who admits he wasn't keen on babies and didn't have much to do with his own during their early years) lost Jackie's esteem, for he had none of the fatherly qualities of support and understanding that she sought.

Twenty or so years later, they are still in conflict, with Jackie now alcoholic, clinging and dependent on Michael, and Michael seeking affection and physical warmth in a passionate affair. Their children find it hard to make and sustain relationships. A footnote to this history is that Michael's brother and Jackie's sister, after their respective divorces, now live together.

The difficulties we will inevitably encounter, when the romantic glow fades and we see the other in the light of reality, can be a step towards a better, more mature relationship, but only if the two partners are able to be sufficiently tolerant and loving to establish the security which will enable them take back their projections, and make themselves into whole personalities; in other words, to grow up.

But if both partners are too needy, deprived or damaged to be able to contain the other while he or she regresses and tries to resolve the issues which have arrested emotional growth, and if their needs swamp each other's, then the original childhood conflict will be perpetuated within the relationship. All the old scenarios will be replayed, all the secret fears of our unacceptability confirmed, and—although slipping down all the old familiar snakes may give an illusion of security—we live out our self-fulfilling prophecies, never believing that things can be any different, yet always hoping for rescue, and repeatedly seeking it from both within our marriage and elsewhere.

Is there any hope for those who emerge from their childhood as emotionally needy and hungry as babies? With divorce increasing and with the rate of births to single women rising, the prospects seem even bleaker for the next generation. What has just been described explains not only many divorces, but many subsequent remarriages as well, and a vicious circle of dissatisfaction.

But the negative cycle *can* be broken—with a determination for dialogue and the communication of our innermost needs, for these can lay the foundation of real acceptance and love, trust and trustworthiness. The journey of marriage *can* help us retrace our steps in our personal journeys; it is our second chance. It is up to us whether we are willing to learn and apply the skills necessary— to take to the road and keep going.

Summary

Our choice of marriage partner is made at three levels. The first two are conscious—we choose for socio-cultural reasons (such as background, interests, education), and we also select for obvious qualities such as physical attraction, attitudes and beliefs. Consciously, we sometimes opt for someone with whom we believe we can achieve something different from the model of our parents' marriage. Nevertheless, our expectations of our married relationship and of the roles of husband and wife within it are strongly influenced by parental and family patterns. The third, unconscious level drives us paradoxically both to seek the security of familiar scenarios—even though these may be painful and destructive—and yet to endeavour to meet needs of which we ourselves are unaware, and which spring from early relationships and situations.

Marriage, and to a certain extent other close relationships during adult life, give both partners the opportunity to re-experience and resolve early relationships which in some way have been inadequate or unsatisfactory. A loving marriage can provide support, nurture, care, patience and tolerance, enabling one or other partner to gain sufficient trust to re-enact these early scenarios constructively, and complete whatever was lacking. The need and attributes which we have repressed in our 'shadow' self and projected onto the spouse have to be reintegrated and 'owned' by us, a process which brings growth and maturity.

We return to the case of Laura, who came to a marriage counsellor because of her deteriorating relationship with Henry.

In counselling, Laura remembered that before her father's death it had been her mother who 'wore the trousers', took the decisions, and handled the finances. She had been a strong and controlling woman, and Laura remembered her father as passive and ineffectual. Through counselling, Laura came to understand that she had longed for the support and protection that her weak and now deceased father had never provided. After her father's death, Laura had been supportive of her mother. But in marrying a man whom she believed could provide qualities of leadership, she was in fact re-enacting the pattern of her family of origin, for her mother too had sought a 'fatherly' husband. Laura realized that she had become the dominant partner in the marriage, for Henry had unconsciously perceived in her a motherly and competent woman, despite the fact Laura was so much younger. His air of maturity and protectiveness was a way of masking (or consigning to his shadow self) his own desire to be mothered and supported, since he had grown up in a family of eight, and his own mother had had little time, leisure or energy to provide the love and nurture he needed.

Can their relationship move forward?

Can they grow within their marriage?

PART II
Ages and Stages

Introduction to Part II

Our life is a journey, a pilgrim path from the womb to the tomb. The view from any one point on this journey will not be the same as from an earlier or a later point, for we are cumulatively shaped and formed by the experiences we undergo en route and the places where we linger. Whether we like it or not, the path leads us onward.

> *Does the road wind up-hill all the way?*
>   *Yes, to the very end.*
> *Will the day's journey take the whole day long?*
>   *From morn to night, my friend.*
>   Christina Rossetti, 'Up-Hill'

We cannot turn back on our life's journey, just as we cannot turn back the clock. We move from infancy to childhood; we grow into adolescents and then young adults; maybe we become parents ourselves; later, we become conscious that our bodies—and perhaps our minds—are not as potent as they were; gradually we release our hold on strength, health and life itself. Whatever tricks we try to play on nature, the process is as unstoppable and inevitable as the mixture of joy and pain it will bring us.

This evolving human process is not merely a physical one: we change and move on in our capacity for learning and reasoning; our emotions develop and our consciousness grows. Socially, morally, spiritually and politically we shall not be the same people at seventy-seven that we were at seven—or even seventeen, thirty-seven or fifty-seven (or if we are, it will be because we have never really lived!). The basic data may remain, but we shall process and handle it differently, add to it, and move on. We do this according to the sequential growth pattern we share with all our fellow human beings, and also according to the unique way in which we have completed the previous legs of the journey, whom we meet on it, whether the road was rough or smooth, and whether we were injured along the way.

Though we can never go back to how we were, or find again the people and the circumstances that time has taken, sometimes we shall discover that the road brings us back to places which seem familiar, to scenes we half recognize, to figures in the landscape with whom we find the security of something long-lost:

Here I was in my sixties, a man with some worldly experience, a distinct sense of irony, given to critical self-observation; and I was shaken with grief like an adolescent. It seemed to me that the tears were not those of the ageing man; inside me, an old self (in fact, a very young self), who might have been considered long dead, was making himself felt as if he still, absolutely, incorrigibly existed. [13]

Unlike the process of our physical growth, maturation and decline, over which we can exercise little control, this journey will offer us choices to make—this road or that? The decisions which send us in one direction or another will be influenced by the map we have been given and by earlier paths, but as we get to know our own capacities and can recognize the signposts, we can choose more freely, even managing to redraw the map or, sometimes, leave it behind. Our growth is seen in the choices we make and how we arrive at them.

Each stage of marriage for each partner parallels one of the stages of child development.
                              Liberty Kovacs, marital therapist [14]

In these next two sections of the book we look at this journey of growth—how our personalities and ways of behaving and relating develop, and how we move on. Those who choose the right travelling companion can gain in strength, be better equipped, learn from mistakes, and weather bad patches and rough going. We also see how we can get stuck at various points—for it can sometimes seem safer and more comfortable to stay put.

We then explore the journey through marriage and how this intimate relationship grows and develops, and see how the places on our individual paths affect and determine what happens when we are travelling together. We also investigate the gateways to new stages of these journeys which can lead us to a new and different affirmation of our self and our relationships, and how to have the fitness and stamina to make the journey.

CHAPTER 3

The Way We Are; the Way We Feel

HOW OUR PERSONALITY DEVELOPS

Our physical growth in our first eighteen or so years is determined not only by the blueprint passed to us through our parents' genes, but also by our activities and our diet and nutrition during formative years. Similarly, our personality develops according to the nurturing and parenting it has received.

The growth of personality

It was Sigmund Freud who formulated one of the best-known theories of phases or stages in the development of a child's personality. He suggested that if the 'tasks' of each stage were not satisfactorily completed by parent and child alike, then this would affect the child both in childhood and in later life, for the personality and emotions would 'arrest' at that point. We have to become sufficiently emotionally fit to move into the next stage. We recognize this when we say that someone is a 'big baby' or that they are 'just one big ego-trip', or when we use the often-quoted but infrequently understood—'he's a typical anal retentive'.

The developmental stages of our babyhood, childhood and adolescence have one principal objective: separating from our parents and becoming an individual, a personality, in our own right. As adults we must achieve the same separation and individuation process in relation to the 'significant other' in our life, for instance in the journey called marriage.

At the same time as our personalities develop in childhood, we also go through parallel and related stages in emotional, cognitive and moral development—how we feel, reason and behave—all of which make us the adults we are when we come into relationship, the two people who have journeyed through life so far to arrive at the point where our paths meet and then merge.

The first three stages in the development of the personality are probably the most significant for the relationships of the future adult, supporting the Jesuit saying, 'Give me a boy till he is seven and I'll show you the man.'

The age of nurture: the oral phase
(0–18 months)
This phase includes our first impressions of the world and what we can expect from it. If these impressions give us love, security and tenderness, we shall grow more likely to expect these and to be able to give them to others. Love is transmitted physically at this time. In the first six months of life our whole being is focused on food, warmth and comfort. Unaware of the world beyond, we are not able to distinguish any division between us and mother, and we live in a blissful and symbiotic union, at one with her and with our experience of her. Our contentment is mother's; her tension will be ours. We signal our needs by making a noise. If they are not met we scream louder, but if we receive consistent and reliable nurture from mother we shall learn in time that, even if she is temporarily absent, what we need will still be provided. So we learn trust, and the 'tasks' of this phase will be completed as time passes. In later life, we will be able to:

♥ trust and depend on others appropriately

♥ cope with frustration reasonably

♥ distinguish fantasy from reality

♥ accept good and bad characteristics
in the same person

♥ achieve a sense of identity and self-worth

♥ accept care from others and thus be able to offer it to others.

If as small babies we are not well served in this, the first great love of our lives, then our adult personalities may be:

♥ demanding, clinging and possessive, in constant fear of being abandoned

♥ capable of violent and destructive anger when frustrated (because these emotions are so powerful and so frightening, we shall project them outside ourselves— making mother into the hateful being. In later life we shall learn to distance any uncomfortable feeling and project it outside ourselves, and the world will seem a hostile place)

♥ withdrawn when situations are painful; given to misinterpreting others' behaviour; prey to day-dreams and delusions

♥ needful of putting some significant others on a pedestal and expecting too much of them while denigrating others

♥ too humble and submissive, unsure of what we have to offer

♥ absorbed in our own concerns to the exclusion of others (though guilty at making demands) and unable to accept intimacy

♥ addicted, specially to what involves putting something (food, drink, cigarettes) in the mouth.

Denise

At thirty-four, Denise had been divorced twice and suffered from bulimia—bingeing on chocolate bars and then purging herself with sometimes more than fifty laxative pills a day. Both her husbands had been violent towards her, and her second husband had left her for another woman while she was in hospital after a suicide attempt. Thereafter a succession of live-in partners mistreated her and then re-enacted the now familiar desertion. Although she came to see clearly the effects that her eating and purging were having on her physical health, and the toll the relationships had taken of her mentally and emotionally, she said she had 'loved' each man and had allowed herself to be humiliated in various ways, begging them not to leave her. She was in great need of support and turned frequently to 'parental' figures such as her vicar and her therapist.

After the age of about six months, babies begin to be able to move away from mother physically, and this process of dissociation accelerates from the age of one year. We start to experience curiosity about the world which, we discover, exists separately from both ourselves and mother, and this results in a good deal of messy exploration, as we test everything the way we know best—by putting it into our mouths. We are increasingly mobile and can feed ourselves, and we begin to be able to make our needs known verbally. The long process of separation and individuation, to be repeated during our intimate adult relationship, has begun.

The 'tasks' the baby, with mother's help, must complete are:

♥ to explore on their own initiative a world that is safe

♥ to be able to control when they leave mother

♥ to separate their feelings from hers

♥ to learn basic concepts about their environment—up/down; near/far; hot/cold

♥ to develop physical co-ordination.

Failure to learn these skills can result in a personality which

♥ is over-adaptive, listless, easily bored and which has difficulty setting goals

♥ is reluctant to take care of needs—physical or emotional, and frequently sustains injury

♥ is unable to take initiative

♥ 'solves' problems inappropriately either by running away from them, doing nothing, or by turning and fighting

♥ uses anger to mask fear.

The age of resistance: the anal phase *(18 months–3 years)*

This is the time when our self-esteem develops (and our sense of satisfaction in our own achievements), for we are now 'separate' from mother in a physical sense. We learn how to apply ourselves to what we undertake, and to persevere in order to succeed. This brings in its wake self-control and self-discipline. But we shall also want to control this universe, of which we find we are no longer the centre, and our 'No! Shan't' and our tantrums are how we do it. Our parents must establish clear and definite boundaries of what is acceptable and what is not, containing them firmly so that these newly discovered energies are not too terrifying. Too much rigidity or protection, however, can lead the child, and later the adult, to become timid and conformist. We have thus to learn how to take appropriate risks and accept authority. These are the beginnings of socialization, and sometimes we shall try and escape its harsh realities by regressing to babyhood, thumb-sucking and clinging.

One way of controlling our world effectively is by deciding whether or not to let go of our faeces while potty-training—hence the label, 'anal retentive'. The answer to this vital question is one that will affect our adult life and relationships to our dying day: 'Who decides?'

If these tasks of beginning to identify the self are not well enough completed, the developing personality can stick here, resulting in

♥ self-criticism, perfectionism, guilt and shame at failure, or

- ♥ an inability to complete tasks, giving up too easily, or sticking with them beyond a reasonable point

- ♥ rigid control of self and/or of others, and an inability to relax

- ♥ over-cautiousness, needing rules and regulations, little spontaneity

- ♥ manipulation of others

- ♥ resentment of authority, either resisting it or submitting to it too easily

- ♥ difficulties with sexual intercourse, which involves 'letting go'.

Nicholas, the businessman we encountered in the previous chapter, had built up his professional world so that he and no one else took the decisions. Lacking in warmth or spontaneity, he controlled his diet and his physical fitness to an obsessive extent. In his personal life he had had superficial relationships in which he was sexually competent, and a former long-term one in which sexual activity had soon ceased. When he met Harriet he found the release of sexual intimacy with the woman he loved difficult. When, at one stage, Harriet took two significant decisions in the relationship without consulting him, Nicholas swiftly took back the power and control by refusing to continue the sexual side of their relationship.

The age of jealousy: the Oedipal-phallic phase

Madeleine

Madeleine was an only child of parents who were also only children, and whose sexual relationship had ceased not long after Maddie's birth. As a child she had been jealous and resentful when her father came home at night; this interrupted her exclusive time with her mother to whom she was very close. In her early twenties, Madeleine had a brief lesbian relationship with a married woman. When her mother died, the adult Madeleine then found it impossible to accept the woman who took her mother's place. In her friendships she had difficulty relating to married couples, preferring to be close to the wives and trying to exclude the husbands, who often felt resentful of this. When she married and had her own two children, one became the favourite and was passionately adored by Maddie while the other was largely ignored, except when used as a go-between in his parents' quarrels.

As toddlers grow into young children, they become aware of, and fascinated by, the physiological differences between mother and father, brother and sister, and they begin to explore their own genitals. This is the age when a young child fantasizes about the parent of the opposite sex, often wanting to marry them, with feelings of intense rivalry towards the same-sex parent. The confusion is often compounded at this age by the arrival of a baby brother or sister, sparking intense feelings of anger, even hatred, of our parents. The strength of these emotions is such that we feel guilt, failure and shame. Unless our parents can reassure us about our personal sense of worth, it will remain in question into adult life.

What is happening is that we are beginning to assume our own sexual identity: the little boy must leave his identification with mother behind for good and begin to model himself on his father; the little girl must identify herself clearly with her mother. This is a vital crossroads in a child's life.

To help children make the right 'choice', and not feed their fantasies about the opposite-sex parent, the mother and father must have a strong relationship themselves, both sexually and emotionally. They must, at this level, be able to exclude the child. If they cannot draw an inviolable boundary round their own relationship, and the child finds itself continuously within the charmed adult circle, then the intense oedipal rivalry will remain, and—like Madeleine—the adult will not be able to cope with triangular situations which recall the rivalry for the affections of one parent, and the jealousy of the other.

If, however, both parents can show that they *are* comfortable with their own sexuality, and are consistent in their dealings with the child, they will avoid seducing the child into any of their own relational difficulties (which can make the child feel responsible for how the parents feel). If father and mother can shoulder their gender roles as the ones who supply and support boundaries and authority, then the child of this age will develop a secure sense of sexual identity, happy with his or her own sexuality. Indeed, when mum and dad model their roles well— shutting the bedroom door, as it were, on their offspring—their children will accept sexual feelings as normal and wholesome, and will be able to integrate them along with other feelings into their adult relationships. Here is a husband from the research sample whose strong marriage inherited much from the model of his parents' physical relationship:

Robert: My parents' room was sacrosanct—if the door was shut. But in the mornings, especially on Saturdays and Sundays, we would all pile into their bed, and our children did with us.

Pattie: But we never took them into our bed apart from that.

Children of such couples will have every chance of growing into adults who enjoy comfortable friendships with the opposite sex, without having to 'sexualize' everything, or use flirtation as the primary means of relating, and who will be able to be competitive in appropriate situations.

However, say for example that the mother 'wears the trousers' and the father is ineffectual or absent. Children can end up confused about gender characteristics, and may become sexually ambivalent.

In other words, if our parents' gender characteristics are unclear, then as adults we may:

♥ feel inadequate as a man or woman and be anxious about demonstrating gender characteristics which may feel too frightening and powerful

♥ inhibit sexual feelings out of fear of rejection

♥ show homosexual tendencies

♥ be jealous of the sexual partner, and unable to cope with everyday threesome situations

♥ put down the opposite sex (*Women! what would you do with 'em?* or *Huh! Typical male!*)

♥ be over-competitive, and fear rivalry from the opposite sex.

The age of belonging: latency
(7–12 years)

There is no major physical change during this period, other than growth. Friends and school become important factors in our lives, and our efforts are oriented towards initiative and achievement. We can become highly competitive and argumentative, while school demands conformity and a surrender to its norms. In return we start to absorb social and moral values from outside the family.

The child in this age range is busy developing skills, belonging to a group, striking deals in the playground, and learning to check and control his or her own behaviour. One of the most vital things we learn from home, peers and school is that we can disagree and the sky will not fall down! Difficulties during this period will produce problems in later life. As adults we may

♥ become perfectionist, rigid, and overly desirous of pleasing (and dissatisfied with our performance)

♥ not know how to complete tasks

♥ have inflexible values

♥ not think things through before taking action.

The age of rebellion: genital/adolescence
(12–18 years)

After the lull of late childhood, the storm breaks—in the trauma of the teens! Bodily changes (some of them troubling and unpleasant, and all of them too obvious) bear witness to the teenager's state of transition. The hormonal changes can bring moodiness and hostility. Interest in the opposite sex grows, with its concomitant sensations of embarrassment, shyness, obsession and rejection. The adolescent may feel self-conscious, uncertain and confused, while appearing insufferably cocky and belligerent. 'Who am I?' is the question that the adolescent must resolve.

Because of these insecurities, adolescents need affection, encouragement and attention. They will often regress to earlier phases, and will simultaneously need to be affirmed in their autonomy and independence and awakening interest in sex, and yet to be loved and nurtured. Teenagers who spend twenty-three hours out of twenty-four in the comforting warmth of their duvets, emerging only to launch tirades of complaint and to eat (for so it seems to many parents), manifest many of the features of babyhood. They may be inarticulate about their needs, or behave in a way which seems counter-productive. And yet their bid for autonomy, the power struggles they have with their parents, and the way their behaviour can control an entire household, have elements of the anal phase as well. All this makes for conflict, both internal and with those around.

At the same time as all this, teenagers must learn a balance between sexual exploration and uncontrolled gratification which, in later life, can be a quest for babyish instant satisfaction and security.

The 'tasks' of adolescents are:

♥ to become independent and able meet their own needs
  in a healthy way

♥ to separate from the family and know that both it and
  they will survive

♥ to complete 'tasks' which were not done before

♥ to structure time

♥ to achieve a balance between needing to belong to a
  group and becoming an individual, between conformity
  and rebellion

♥ to move from the dependency of childhood through teenage independence to an eventual interdependence (separate from the family but able to reintegrate when necessary and appropriate)

♥ to affirm that their basic life position is OK.

If this does not happen, then as adults we may:

♥ continue to seek and use others to meet our needs

♥ continue to play sexual games

♥ become unable to form intimate relationships

♥ be either extremely dependent or exceptionally rebellious in later life.

Return trips

In adult life, however mature and well adjusted we are, there will be times when we need to return to an earlier point on the journey. It is almost invariably true that 'under stress we all regress': when ill we want to be babied; when in love we seek oneness with the beloved; when hurt we want comfort. These return trips are instinctual and spring from our mechanism for survival. If they can be recognized and tolerated by us and by those close to us for as long as is necessary (but no longer) we shall know ourselves better and grow from that knowledge. Here the author Edward Blishen describes his feelings during a first visit to India at the age of sixty-eight:

> *The fact was that being close to seventy, as we both were, had all the marks of a much-earlier phase in our lives: adolescence. That was a time you felt gauchely new to the place, terribly eager to cut an impressive dash and terribly aware that you were not able to do so: and when the world seemed to be boiling under your feet. Nothing was what it had seemed, and everything you clapped eyes on was in a state of beautiful and alarming transition... Everything was engaged in turning into something else.*[15]

If for whatever reason some vital ingredient is missing in the parenting of children, especially up to the age of seven, and a 'task' has not therefore been completed well enough, then this can have a profound effect on the future adult.

However, it does not take dramatic, out-of-the-ordinary events for this to happen and cause the personality to 'arrest' emotionally at some point, for certain children seem to be born more needy than others. For instance, it is only within the last twenty years or so that health authorities have understood that if a very young child is separated from its mother through the hospitalization of either then a severe and lasting deprivation can result. The effects may not be visible and it may seem that the child has recovered from the experience, but both as child and adult that person may lack the ability to entrust themselves in relationships and may be unwilling to be emotionally vulnerable. As we saw in the last chapter, some people seek desperately to find someone who will supply what was missing, but may be so mistrustful that they do not know how to accept or receive love. Similarly, the child whose parents did not have a strong and secure relationship is likely to repeat the geometry when they become a parent, by relating inappropriately to their child in a way which should be reserved for the spouse.

The Way We Behave

WHAT MOTIVATES OUR BEHAVIOUR AND DECISIONS

At the same time as we develop our psychosexual side, we learn to complete other 'tasks'. How we do so (or not) will also affect the way we relate to others—colleagues, friends, organizations, employers, society in general and—perhaps most importantly— our partner. We do not always advance in some areas at the same pace as we do in others, so that people who have the moral and social maturity to hold down responsible jobs, and even make life-and-death decisions, may not necessarily have attained a high degree of affective maturity. For example, someone may be a highly competent doctor or teacher, in whose hands the welfare and well-being of others reside, and yet that same person may be badly in need of warmth, support and nurture. The example of numerous MPs during the 1980s and 1990s spring to mind in this respect; equally, research suggests that many priests and ministers seek ordination precisely because holy *Mother* Church seems to offer security and belonging.[16]

The way we behave and relate

How do we choose between right and wrong? How do we define these concepts? Do they change as we move on through life? Does our gender make any difference to our actions?

The changes in our perspective on issues of right and wrong, and on justice and the law, as we progress from childhood to adulthood are fixed in their order, and we cannot move forward to the next phase of our moral development until we have completed the previous one. As in the development of our

73

personality, we may become stuck at any one point, and this also will contribute to how we make choices and decisions, and how we resolve conflict and dilemmas.

What is morality?

Many people see the term 'morality' as a negative one, something which equals 'should' and 'ought', denying and stifling spontaneity and the true expression of our personality— a sort of 'hardening of the oughteries', as Gerard Hughes SJ puts it in his best-selling *God of Surprises*. But if we understand morality to be the way we relate and behave to other people, it can affirm life and self rather than deny them. For instance, 'should' and 'ought' are irrelevant judgments on parents who are not emotionally mature enough to listen to their child, hear its distress, comprehend its desires, and meet its needs. And while we do not actually have to condone the single teenage mother who, alone in the squalor of a vandalized tower block, batters her infant, we do need to understand the roots of her action, and know that the seeds of it are in ourselves as well.

'Morality', the way we behave, evolves with us, and is more a matter of motivation than of prohibition and authority. It is not something fixed, but is inextricably linked to our development as people, to our ability to trust, to accept, to see others' needs, to be independent, and to take initiative—in short, to our personality and the past that has shaped it.

Some questions of 'morality'...

- Do you 'have sex' with your girlfriend/boyfriend whenever you feel the urge?

- Does fear of pregnancy/AIDS stop you going the whole way?

- Would you have sex, even though worried about getting pregnant/AIDS, because everyone else does and you're the last virgin in the class?

- Or because you thought you'd lose your girlfriend/boyfriend if you didn't?

- Do religious rules stop you having an affair?

- Is sex always part of a loving, committed relationship? Even if it's between two men or two women?

- Who decides?

- How do you decide?

or again—

- Do you always obey the speed limit?

- Would you drive up a motorway at 90 mph if you were sure you would not be caught?

- Would you drive up a motorway at 90 mph because your spouse had just landed at the airport and you were desperate to see them after two months apart?

- Would you drive up a motorway at 90 mph because your friends were calling you a wimp?

- Do you accelerate over the legal speed limit to avoid someone driving dangerously?

- Would you drive at 90 mph if you had a sick child in the back and were trying to get to the hospital?

- How do you decide?

Our honest answers to these questions reveal the point we have reached on our journey.

Pre-morality

As we saw earlier, infants do not distinguish between where their world ends and their mother's begins. There is no outside world, so no concept of right and wrong. Contentment feels good, hunger or discomfort feel bad, and it is therefore impossible to spoil a tiny baby, and pointless to punish. Under extreme stress—perhaps severe illness or pain, trauma or bereavement—an adult may behave like a very small baby.

The first two steps in the journey are essentially self-centred.

Punishment and obedience

I mustn't be late; the missus will kill me!

The very young child's perception of good and bad, right and wrong, will depend entirely on the consequence of its actions. If we're caught and punished because we broke a cup/ate the sweets/kicked the dog, then what we did also feels bad. If nobody tells us off, then the act was OK. The world is seen in relation to our ego. Many grown-up people act like this about their income tax, drink-driving, dropping litter, fiddling expenses, or adultery.

The transition to the next step will come when we can grasp that what we need and want is not necessarily what everybody else needs or wants.

Egoism

Unless you're nice to me, I'm going out!

At this stage (usually around four to six years old), children's actions are still primarily motivated by selfishness, though they now understand that other people's feelings are different from their own. Their motivation, and thus what is 'right', is still the satisfaction of their own needs, although they will undertake apparently unselfish actions which spring from pure self-interest. For example, they may help mother, but only because they think they will get a sweetie or a treat for being 'good'. So human relationships are seen in terms of 'You scratch my back and I'll scratch yours.' In adult life many business and political affairs are conducted, and marriages will often be based, on this principle. Superficially the relationship may work smoothly, but will be shallow and will founder in a crisis since the partners are ultimately concerned only with themselves.

Transition to the next two steps on the journey, will come as children are progressively 'socialized' as a result of spending more time away from the family. They come to see that the needs of other people are often in conflict with their own.

Peer pressures

Look, darling, I've cooked your favourite meal!

When we go to school we learn new values. Our self-centredness is slowly replaced by a dawning awareness of the feelings, rights and concerns of others. We now want other people's approval, and we are motivated to please and help them. In adult life, those whose behaviour is at this stage will set great store by fulfilling their obligations to their spouse, family, social circle or colleagues. We can now understand not only that someone else sees things differently from us, but that our own actions, nice or nasty, may bring similar ones in return—'If I do this to you, you'll do it to me.' Relationships become important factors in deciding what actions to take and we start to discern the motivations behind other people's behaviour. Similarly, we hope to be kindly judged ourselves.

But as we move forward, we learn that conforming to group expectations in order to be acceptable and accepted may bring us into conflict with other social groups—our family, the law, the church. For example, we have sex 'because it's hard to be the only virgin left at seventeen', or we have that extra one for the road before driving home because we don't want our mates to think we're wet.

This theory of stages—in the way we behave and its motivation (our moral development)—was formulated by Lawrence Kohlberg[17] according to the responses of boys and men to various dilemmas. But it poses a problem because many women will never go beyond this stage of wanting to please, being less orientated towards abstract principles of justice. A more recent theory by Carol Gilligan[18] suggested that women are more motivated by responsibility, sensitivity, and care of others. For many women, dilemmas arise more often from competing responsibilities than from opposing principles. The woman trapped in the unfulfilling marriage where she may suffer verbal, even physical, abuse may view her options as between the responsibilities to her children and her husband—and maybe also herself.

Law and order

But I have to go on the course, it's company rules.

As we move on, good actions will come to be motivated more by respect for authority, doing one's duty and obeying the rules and the law, without questioning why this should be so. Many adults never progress beyond this stage: 'Slow down, you're over the speed limit'; 'Our policy is never to give a refund'; 'Abortion is wrong—the Pope says so'; 'You're not allowed to park there.' Moral right is reflected in the laws to which society, organizations, and even households and families are subject, even if there may be other pressing considerations.

Raphael and Emma

Raphael and Emma were in their late thirties. Raphael was a solicitor and Emma worked for the director of a large company. Raphael was Jewish, and rigidly followed traditional Jewish law, including dietary and other rules. He would do exactly what he was told by those in authority, and the rabbi was an important figure in his life. Emma was far more liberal, and as their marriage progressed she found Raphael's focus on rules and regulations increasingly intrusive in their domestic life.

Raphael's mother was a forceful personality; she dominated her son and followed the couple when they moved from London to Lancaster. Raphael always supported his mother rather than his wife, because respect for his mother was one of the rules by which he lived. This caused enormous resentment, frustration and anger in Emma, who thought her mother-in-law ruled their entire life and marriage. The breakthrough came only after two years of counselling, when Raphael could understand what his wife was going through. However, it took only this one shift in his perspective to change him and the whole relationship. Raphael was enabled to see that his strict adherence to 'what was right' was not, in fact, right for his wife or his marriage. The counsellor-client relationship also enabled

him to relate to a figure of 'authority' whom he could respect but who did not hand out rules about his behaviour.

If we start to question the rightness of a rule in a particular
case, or see that sometimes its implementation is not always
beneficial, we may move on to a point where the greater good
will be the motivation for our action.

Social contract

Let's take it in turns to wash up.

If we have grown up securely, and if we have separated emotionally
from our home and family of origin, if we are mature—being
neither childishly dependent nor rebelliously adolescent for the
sake of it—then we shall have internalized certain standards of
right and wrong. We may then come to realize that sometimes,
although the reason for a rule or law is valid, at times it can be at
variance with the needs of society (or a particular group or the
relationship). We understand, however, that we are part of that
society, and we shall have a grasp of how it works and what made
it the way it is. If it is dysfunctional, we shall be able to work from
within to change what prevents it working well. We can be flexible
in our own views, principles and needs, though this may mean that
the 'rules' have to be relaxed. In marriage and relationship, this will
produce a willingness to resolve difficult issues by negotiation. The
people and couples who reach this point are open to change,
flexible, and can distinguish between personal freedom and the
good of the majority.

The ideal

*Sue's job will benefit us all, though it will make things
more hectic at home.*

In terms of moral development, not many people manage to
maintain the ideal position consistently, for it involves seeing
beyond the differences between people and systems to the

79

unity which they may share. Ecumenism, the unity between different church denominations, is an example of the maturity of being able to see further than what separates. Here, what is good and morally right is motivated by the deeply-held beliefs and values which we ourselves have chosen. Thus some of us choose to break the law in our hunger for justice, equality, peace, dignity and human rights, for we shall be operating on the principles underlying the law—its spirit rather than its letter. Conscientious objectors, suffragettes and nuclear weapons protesters may have been operating on this level, though there may undoubtedly have been some of their number whose motivation was less altruistic. Jesus cut through differences and blind obedience to rules and called his followers to something which transcends these—the kingdom of God.

In marriage, the mature love of two spouses—at whatever age—will enable them to leave behind stereotypical roles and expectations, for the common bond of trust and freedom enable them to do this, as Cassandra Jardine notes in 'The worm's turn to make the tea' in the *Daily Telegraph* of 27 December 1994:

No longer are house husbands necessarily self-conscious New Men, caring and sharing as a form of image-preening, nor are they gloomy unemployed ones who would rather be out at work. Engineers, graphic designers, stage managers, pilots, big hulking men with deep voices and healthy sexual self-images are taking over the traditional female roles. Talking to a selection of them, they appear happy and well adjusted, enjoying their work and not caring a jot whether anyone says they are wimps.

How we move on

Throughout our life we are constantly evolving. Crisis is the springboard of change. The turning point or decisive moment will come when we confront a problem or task which calls for a new way of reacting, reasoning, deciding. Conflict, which is the inevitable and necessary concomitant of being in relationship—with spouse, lover, family, group, organization, employer or society—produces the moment of tension, and if we can respond creatively to it we grow and move on. This is a process that we recognize in ourselves only retrospectively when we look back and see how we have changed.

But change is more painful than complacency, and involves the loss of something—or someone—we have clung to: a parent is terminally ill and dies; a spouse is made redundant; a secret is discovered; a child is in trouble; a friend has a breakdown; there is widowhood, divorce. These and the lesser everyday conflicts and crises call us forward to act and react in different ways. People will often say they did not grow up till circumstances of death, desertion, divorce or other drama forced them to. The miners' strike in Britain in the early 1980s threatened many women with the prospect of penury, a change of lifestyle, and a dispirited husband permanently at home. For the first time, many found within themselves resources of courage, initiative and intelligence they had not dreamed of.

An essential truth suddenly or gradually becomes more important than fear of the future, and we are both spurred and freed to move on.

If we are willing to make life's journey one of discovery of our inner self, and not be content with the surface and the superficial, if we can explore who we are and why we behave as we do, then each step can bring a transition in how we feel, think, behave and react which will bring us closer to the fulfilment of that self. Paradoxically this involves both looking back at the landscape of the journey so far and a willingness to enter unknown territory. The next chapter looks at this paradox: at how the route we have travelled can direct the journey of marriage, and how marriage can help us redraw the map.

The Marriage Workout

'WE'RE DOING IT TOGETHER'

Because marriage is something dynamic and ever changing, whose process parallels that of the years between birth and leaving home, it will revisit places which seem familiar to us on our individual journey. This chapter is an attempt to chart the sequence and the main characteristics of the process of marriage, and the following chapters will describe each stage in greater detail, noting what may impede progress and what will promote movement.[15]

Jen and Darren

Jen and Darren came for counselling when they were in their early thirties and had been married for fourteen years. They had met as teenagers, both from family backgrounds where there had been little affirmation or affection. Darren idolized Jen, and she was flattered by the idealistic picture he had of her, for her self-esteem was low.

The romance faded quickly for Jen when she realized the extent of the control Darren had over her: she was not allowed to take decisions or to have much of a life of her own. One night she went out to a club dinner and came home later than planned. Darren was convinced she was having an affair. Both entered a phase of 'reality'—seeing the other in the light of truth rather than the flattering glow of romance. Jen learned to manipulate Darren by feeding his suspicions, and tremendous conflict erupted, often with physical violence from both sides.

Gradually Jen became stronger, took an interest in her

appearance and started jogging, and Darren was forced to recognize the change in the woman he had married. Through counselling they started negotiating what they wanted of each other, and at a practical level they started to decide together where they should go on holiday, how they should spend Christmas. They finally achieved a more equal footing in their relationship, though Jen was still happy in many ways to let Darren have much of the final responsibility for decisions.

Jen and Darren illustrate the six stages which characterize relationships which, through difficulty and discord, effort and pain, move forward.

With our unique characteristics, quirks, gifts and wounds, our personalities develop. We have seen that in certain areas of our life this development will 'freeze' at a certain point if the tasks of that stage of the journey have not been well enough completed. However much we may rationalize, intellectualize, disguise and sanitize our emotions and reactions, our decisions and choices, they will remain those of that particular stage. They will influence all our undertakings, and the greatest effect will be seen in our closest adult relationships.

Many of us perceive marriage as something static between two unchanging people, as one newly-wed interviewee explained:

I'd like to think each of us is the same. That's why we are such good friends. If we could stay that way we'd have a great marriage.
                    The Beginning of the Rest of Your Life

But we do change, and our partner's perception of us changes, too, to the point where one or other can feel there has been a betrayal or violation of the original deal: 'You're not the person I married any longer!' is the cry of a bewildered and hurt human being, and it heralds many a bitter marital wrangle. But we do change, and our partner's perception of us changes, too.

Unfinished business

Whether married or in a permanent committed relationship, being a couple implies a process together which unfolds through time and which, like life itself, brings with it tasks to be mastered at each stage. An enduring intimate relationship—and marriage is still for many people the most significant—offers the adult the opportunity to tackle the 'unfinished business', the tasks which may have been inadequately completed in the course of childhood and adolescence. This is especially true of our earliest years which are the footings and foundations of all future relationships. If these issues can be satisfactorily resolved, both the marriage and the individuals will continue growing and developing, and the relationship will be constantly (but not necessarily consciously) redesigned according to the needs of both partners. If, however, partners cannot fulfil each other's needs, then the conflicts of early life will well up and will block the couple's progress, becoming one of the largest 'snakes' on the board of marriage down which the couple will slide again and again.

In other words, marriage can be our second chance to find all that was missing earlier in our lives in our relationship with our parents, enabling us to be sure enough of ourselves and of who we are to become individuals and yet to live in harmony with other human beings. After we have left our family of origin, our marriage becomes the bridge between the individual and the outside world, and this is part of its social perspective. The 'tasks' of marital growth and development echo the childhood processes of growth and separation from our parents, and mirror what we have to accomplish in all our adult relationships: a balance between dependence and independence, closeness and distance. Life, from the cradle to the grave, is about learning to be separate but together.

Forward or back?

Just as individuals can arrest during the growth of their personality, so the couple can stick at any stage of the developmental process of their marriage. Similarly they may need to redo or relearn a particular task, for it is true also of coupledom that under stress we all regress: absence, illness, bereavement and trauma can all bring about the need to run back and shelter in a past age. Everybody does this to some extent, and it can enrich a marriage by bringing to it renewed closeness, trust, and acceptance. The insight and awareness gained in redoing earlier tasks, or visiting earlier places on the marriage 'map', can mean that some of the pitfalls can be avoided in future.

But in any crisis there is always a choice: we can sit back and wallow and stick in our problems, or take the opportunity to rework past conflicts and situations—'unfinished business'. The relationship of husband and wife, indeed any close human bond, will not develop automatically. It requires, above all, the will of both partners to make things work; it needs negotiation of endless compromise, tolerance of individual differences, and a working out of how appropriate the demands of each partner are. But if the commitment to each other and to the relationship is there, then *anything*—the disasters, the rows, the pettinesses, even the infidelities—is redeemable. With commitment, patience, love, endurance, kindness, and sometimes with outside help, we can rescue our actions, and perhaps our marriage, from the mess in which they might otherwise end up.

Getting stuck

The length of time a particular stage takes can vary, and husband and wife may themselves grow at different speeds. If we have not learned trust, and if our self-esteem has never been fostered by unconditional love—either from our parents or our partner—then change can seem too threatening, demanding or painful. Instead of using stress, tension and problems as springboards for growth, one or both partners will protect themselves against change, fleeing from it, avoiding it, resisting it and withdrawing as much as possible from painful situations. But even after years of stagnation and inertia it will sometimes take only the tiniest shift of attitude from one partner to start the couple moving on again.

Parenthood

The process never stops, though for many years of the marriage there are likely to be others alongside the couple when the birth of children or the care of elderly relatives add to the size of the household. Children will inevitably produce change and tension within a marriage. They may represent a further loss of independence in a young couple struggling to come to terms with the fact that marriage was not perhaps a passport to autonomy; their advent may set off jealousy in a partner who feels unloved or deprived; or they may reawaken imperfectly resolved oedipal issues in husband or wife. The fact that young married couples are now choosing to reproduce later [19] may prolong for them the earliest 'romantic' stage of marriage, making reality consequently harder to confront when the time comes.

In fact, the developmental 'journey' of marriage[20] can also apply to many other kinds of long-term relationship. We can see the same patterns recurring in our relationships with friends, organizations, employers, the church, and so on. We can sometimes recycle through all the stages according to the need of the moment. For instance, this can happen when two friends meet after a period apart: they will move sequentially through all the stages in a few hours. Those familiar with groups will see a parallel between the forming, storming, norming and performing of groups and the path from dependence through independence to interdependence.

Romance

Just as the tiny baby knows nothing of the outside world and is blissfully at one with its mother, so the couple who fall in love have eyes only for each other. Isolated and insulated from reality in the newness and intensity of relationship, the world for them takes on the glow of their feelings through which every experience is filtered. It may not be quite true that 'everybody loves a lover', but lovers themselves experience a fullness of emotion which wells up and overflows, giving them the impression of having love enough to spare for the whole world.

As we saw in Chapter 2, new lovers are entranced by each other, for they see the completion of themselves reflected in the beloved's eyes; they have found their other half and their sameness unites them. During courtship they are with each

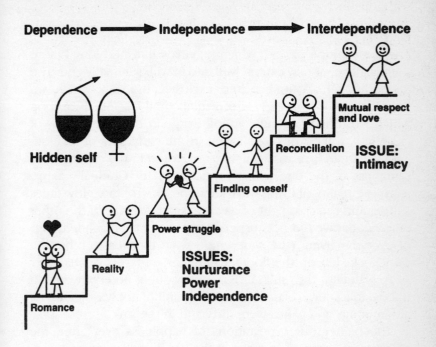

other as often as possible, and emotional partings and reunions sustain the novelty at a high-octane level. They are intoxicated by being in love, sometimes more than by each other. Romance often finds its expression in frequent love-making. Expectations that this is how life will be, that this time perfection will last, are high.

But these are the fantasies of passion, and marriages based on them alone are built on sand. These rose-coloured dreams that characterize the beginning of relationship are, however, as necessary a part of the early days of marriage as are the hours of warmth, milk and safety for the infant in its mother's arms. The need at this stage is for nurturing, and—just as the infant 'learns' to trust in order to be able to receive and later give care—if enough is provided then firm foundations will have been laid for a mutually caring, gratifying and supportive relationship separate from the family of origin.

Reality

The honeymoon period, which may have finished long before the marriage, or may extend well into it, will eventually end. The unconditional acceptance and exclusive intimacy which we knew at mother's breast, which fulfilled all our needs and on which we touch fleetingly and illusorily in the first ecstasy of closeness, will never come again. In the early days of relationship we are in love with ourselves mirrored in the other, in the sameness of the one who was made for us. Gradually as we learn the reality of living with someone, the roseate glow fades a little, and the cold light of day breaks in. Aspects of the other emerge that we did not suspect, from the small niggling things of everyday living (the squeezing of the toothpaste tube, the dirty socks left on the floor), to unguessed facets of character (the jealousy, the sulks). For one couple interviewed, an unbearable source of discord was his habit of not washing up till all the mugs and plates were dirty and in the sink.

The higher our expectations of happiness ever after, the greater our sense of let-down at the banality of everyday living. The more we put our lover on a pedestal of perfection as the one who can solve everything for us, the angrier we shall be when we glimpse the feet of clay. Disappointment, disillusion and differences can well up, and although early in marriage we may try to disguise these and avoid disagreements, we cannot do so for ever. Conflict and tension are part of relationship, and are not a reflection of the inadequacy of our partner, ourselves or of the marriage.

The challenge now is to accommodate and adapt to reality, and to let go of any fantasies we may have that the relationship can fulfil all our needs. If we try to deny the fact that harmony no longer prevails all the time, if we distort differences and evade conflict, then real problems will arise, for we shall no longer be communicating the reality of ourselves to the other.

The relationship will not progress, and one partner may try either to woo or coerce the other back to the idyll of their romance.

This is a difficult and complex time in a relationship, requiring the resolution of several apparent paradoxes: husband and wife must compromise to achieve their individual needs; they must deal with conflict and yet remain close; they must preserve their togetherness but begin to re-establish links with the outside world of friends and family; and the relationship must grow as a twosome but still allow the individuals in it to learn to be more independent of each other. To add to the complexities and inconsistencies of this stage of the journey, it often occurs around the time when the first child is born. The needs and expectations of baby and partner can be incompatible, and in the midst of all this the couple has to find its way ahead both as individuals and as a couple, in a relationship which encompasses everyone's needs and expectations, including their own.

Power struggle

The struggle to be our own person while being part of a couple is at its height during this post-romance phase of the journey. It is a time when the couple's interests are becoming increasingly divergent and there can be a strong desire for independence and autonomy on the part of one or both—for instance when a non-earning partner resumes or starts work outside the home, perhaps for the first time having money to spend and tasting the freedom offered by a different perspective on life. This can threaten the other partner who, perhaps because they are at a point in personal development where they still fear abandonment, may react strongly and violently against any such move. One husband seen during counselling said he would 'allow' his wife to get a job on condition that everything was done at home exactly how, and at precisely the same time, as it had always been.

When both partners are finding new directions and interests outside the relationship there may be a huge conflict, with both stubbornly asserting their new-found identity, afraid that compromise could be seen as surrender. The result can be that an emotional gulf opens up between them. It can be a time of anger and bitterness, with accusations that it is the other partner who wants to stifle growth and freedom, the other who must change, and that they should never have married. If disappointment runs high and the distance between the couple grows, then an affair may start in order to meet unmet needs, or as a bid for autonomy, or as a way of getting back at the other.

By this time the partners will know each other well, and there will be few facets of the personality which remain hidden—which can provide the verbal ammunition for a row. The couple must now acknowledge, and begin to accept and respect, both the positive and the negative aspects of the other (which, as we saw in Chapter 3, will not be easy for someone who received unreliable nurture during the first year or so of life). If the relationship is to move forward the partners need to make a positive commitment to it, and to each other. They must develop a mutual caring and respect, and be able to put themselves in the other's shoes and see the other's perspective. This requires a stage in our moral development which reaches beyond that of the small child.

Finding ourselves

The average length of a marriage at divorce is less than ten years.

Nevertheless, nearly a quarter of all divorces in the UK occur later on—between the sixteenth and the twenty-fifth year of marriage.[21]

These middle years of marriage echo the confusion and struggle of the adolescent, at a time when a husband and wife may be dealing with just such issues in their own children. Now the conflict between dependence and independence reaches its height and, just as the teenager needs to regress to earlier stages, so the married couple may need to resolve issues from the past. 'Who am I?' is once again their urgent question, which may become more pressing as their own parents die. The death of a parent should never be underestimated in the effect it may have on an adult child's life; it is often the springboard to self-discovery and a change of direction.

The psychologist Carl Jung defined the tasks of mid-life as:

♥ bringing more and more of our unconscious, of our shadow self, into consciousness, so that our true personalities may blossom;

♥ recentring our life around a new set of values;

♥ redirecting the energies that have been used in coping with life in order to foster inner growth.

Personal needs and wants, rather than those of the relationship, now take precedence. Just as adolescents begin to discover their identity and to move away from the family, so a person in the middle years of marriage may perceive that their true self may find fulfilment only away from the relationship which is now perceived as stifling and imprisoning.

Not surprisingly, this is a period when separation and divorce are talked about, and sometimes become realities. As parents must allow teenagers a long rein so they can answer the question 'Who am I?', this stage often requires one partner to invest a great deal of trust and commitment in the marriage. One woman in her late forties, whose children had now left home, spent eighteen months in a part of the country where her family roots were, some 300 miles away from her husband, training as a social worker and living in what amounted to a commune with other women. This was breaking out with a vengeance from her most traditional of marriages, but she and her husband managed to maintain a degree of connectedness during this time, meeting every other weekend. Although her husband hated the time apart, it saved their marriage and helped it grow. She eventually returned to him, and then she and her husband retired to the area where she had 'escaped' to, and she continued to work there as a social worker.

If, as that couple did, spouses consciously choose their relationship as a way of life, if they are able to be independent and yet reconnect (just as adolescents move away from the family but can eventually come home for weekends), and if they have learned to negotiate and resolve conflict, then the marriage can move onwards, with the individuality of each partner accepted and respected. But there are plenty of snakes in this part of the board, and often they will come from outside the relationship as much as from within. We have mentioned the death of parents; there are also the stresses of ageing parents and in-laws; of redundancy; of moving house; of difficulties with the children; and of the 'empty nest' syndrome, where partners have to face each other without the comforting security of their parental role (when we have been parents for twenty or so years the question 'Who am I?' can seem both urgent and brutal). And, of course, one place to 'find ourselves'—or at least our former selves—may be in the eyes of a lover.

All these occurrences figure high in the hierarchy of stress. Husband and wife will be able to move on if they can cope with stress as a team, support each other and recognize each other's strengths.

Working through

Once through this perilous point in the marital process, the couple will be less inclined to blame each other, less concerned only for themselves, and will find pleasure in giving to each other. There are echoes here of the 'social contract' phase of moral development, where the individual is committed to a social group (in this case, the marriage) and will work from within to change it by flexibility and negotiation. Personal freedom has been achieved, but it can be relinquished at times when it is for a greater good.

Indeed, within the marriage there may now be a recognition that differences can enhance rather than threaten the relationship. All aspects of the partner's personality, including their limitations are now accepted, leading to more realistic expectations and an appreciation of the strengths of both the partner and of the relationship. There is more sharing of responsibilities, jobs and decisions, and if all the tasks of this stage have been accomplished well enough then the couple will appreciate their freedom from the ties of children.

Trust, or tolerance—or both—grow. A partner's friends of

the opposite sex do not seem so threatening. Ideally, the couple have now achieved interdependence, taking responsibility for themselves and their own behaviour, but with greater mutual acceptance and with increased warmth and intimacy.

Collaboration

Fully accepted and fully accepting, the couple can relax from trying to please, to do the right thing, from worrying what the other is thinking or how they will react. Secure in this knowledge, man and wife are free to grow, to explore new ways of fulfilling themselves and to be creative (instead of pouring so much energy into the marriage), for they know they can separate and reconnect without losing their identity. Jung defined the characteristics of old age as:

♥ reaping the benefits of the inner quest of mid-life;

♥ pursuing this inwardness to foster integrity, wholeness;

♥ looking forward to a new birth in death.

It is, of course, never as simple or as ideal as that. The later years of a marriage can bring great upheaval: retirement, reduced income, failing body and mind, isolation and fear. When confronting such crises, couples in later life will need to recycle through the earlier stages when facing loss (through illness, redundancy or retirement, bereavement). They will go through yet another sequence—that of mourning. But if they have completed their own developmental and marital phases adequately then the losses will be met, tackled, coped with and integrated with less difficulty than if they had never achieved the fulfilment of their personality, never been able to answer the question 'Who am I?', never become independent. If they have learned early on both to give and receive care and nurture, then acceptance of help in old age will come more naturally; if trust has been engendered throughout life, then abandonment by death will not be the end of the world; if love and respect have been fostered and other people valued and accepted, then the prospect of life ending may not be so terrifying.

This is a brief run-through, or a small-scale map which charts and outlines the main landmarks of the journey through a marriage which husband and wife have been emotionally fit enough to undertake. No marriage moves smoothly on quite like this. Each is unique, and its uniqueness comes from the two people and their personalities, their problems and their pasts, their potential and their gifts. Each marriage will lose its way, go up blind alleys, have to turn back and find different directions, redo parts of the route, run out of petrol and get punctures, even meet accidents, crashes, and teeter on the edge of precipices. Each will also have its own solutions, its own unique ways of handling what comes along.

Having a map, however, helps us even more in the general direction of our journeys, and it also tells us that others have passed that way on their own pilgrimages, travelling through similar difficulties and joys. In the 'snakes and ladders' metaphor, no couple will get across the board without encountering, and going down, some pretty big snakes. What we must remember is that it is normal to be where we are at any given moment, even if the place is painful and hard.

This sequence of 'stages', which we explore in greater detail in the next six chapters, helps us know how to recognize what is happening in the process of being a couple, and how we can best limber up for it.

CHAPTER 6

Romance

'IT'S A LOT OF FUN'

What do small children need from their parents in order to grow and become independent? When asked this question, interviewees replied:

♥ time

♥ touch

♥ admiration

♥ encouragement

♥ acceptance

♥ continuity

♥ a sense of belonging

♥ security

♥ satisfaction

♥ pleasure of play

♥ feeding

♥ nurture.

If we look at the behaviour of a couple who are deeply in love and at the beginning of their commitment to each other, we see that the list above constitutes the very things that characterize their courtship and the early days of their marriage. A baby and the mother who embraces him in her arms look into each other's eyes in mutual gratification. So it is with lovers: 'Thus long in mutual bliss they lay embraced,' wrote Geoffrey Chaucer. Even their vocabulary reflects the parallel between the two periods of life: baby talk, pet names, and sometimes merely inarticulated noises of pleasure. The warmth, tenderness and pleasure of infancy are re-enacted, with constant touch and caressing. As mother and baby are enwrapped in their relationship, so the lovers have eyes for no one else: they are fused in their oneness and togetherness. The outside world does not exist. We have all witnessed the embrace of a couple which excludes the rest of humanity—on station platforms, in the high street, on the beach, in the cinema.

The idyll

It is exclusive; it is romanticized and idealized, close and intense; it is the chance for fun and fantasy:

> *It was apple blossom time. We did all sorts of fun things, didn't we, in those first months? It was brilliant. It was exciting.*

One couple literally shut themselves off from the world when they were first married:

> *The first year we were married we were on board the boat. When we did come ashore we did lots of cycling and walking and running and skiing and kayaking. We had great fun. We were happy. I felt more secure.*

The honeymoon period provides an ideal other world shielded and sheltered from the harshness of reality... 'a wedding journey, the express object of which is to isolate two people on the ground that they are all the world to each other', as George Eliot describes it in *Middlemarch*. Just as with the symbiotic oneness of mother and child, so the two lovers seem to merge their personalities, and may develop the same values, interests, habits, thoughts, feelings and ideas. 'Togetherness' is the name many give it. Each responds to the other with the powerful empathy of the mother for her baby. Their sameness is emphasized, and they are often blind to any differences between them.

Some of the couples interviewed in the Mansfield and Collard book, *The Beginning of the Rest of your Life?*, illustrate the characteristics of the romance of the early days of life together:

You're together—you're one not two—you're not on your own.

Togetherness—doing things together—being able to talk to him about anything.

Sleeping together, not sex, sharing all our life together.

Having someone around all the time—someone to fall back on—someone to come home to.

One couple, happily married for some twenty-nine years, described the 'togetherness' of their first year of marriage:

Wife: It was a great year, wasn't it? It shouldn't necessarily have been because we were in a bedsit in Brighton. We had one room with a shower in it and a shared bathroom, and a loo down the hall and a small sort of passage called a kitchen, and we had fun. It was just us, and we were very happy.

Husband: And there was a Belling two-bar fire and a heater that took coins, and we lived on bacon bits.

Wife: We just did fine. We were very happy.

Boundaries
This sort of loving and exclusive atmosphere builds a secure base from which the relationship can grow and move forward. The establishment of a good sexual relationship (which itself mirrors the 'oneness' of mother and baby) helps give the couple a clear sense of identity separate from the family of origin, and gives them the chance to forge the bonds of marriage. For this reason couples need boundaries which protect them from the intrusion of the outside world. In the days when young marrieds used to live with one set of parents,

unbearable strains were put on their as-yet fragile relationships. The archetypal comic figure and butt of many jokes—the interfering mother-in-law—could and still can be a real source of marital discord.

But how do men and women marrying for the second time, after divorce or widowhood, establish their couple identity? They have to create an identity as a couple which is separate from their personal histories and past relationships, but at the same time they must recognize and acknowledge that the past is always present, for it shapes us and moulds our present reactions. If the widow(er) or divorcee has been a single parent for some time, the process of separating from past relationships will be a difficult and delicate one, for to a certain extent that relationship must be kept alive for the sake of the children who sprang from it. There will almost inevitably be friction when the couple try to erect a firm boundary round their relationship, for the children of the previous union will probably be accustomed to having an exclusive place with the parent they live with. Nevertheless, now is the time when a store of trust, respect and support must be built on which the couple can draw in times of difficulty, change and stress. In our metaphor of the journey, now is the time to get a full tank of petrol and provisions for the road ahead.

Thus the beginning of the couple's identity is formed now, and how well they cope with the journey and weather the storms will depend on the quality of this time, during which they must accomplish certain 'tasks'.

The tasks of Stage 1

■ to build the foundation of a relationship which for both is gratifying, caring and supportive

■ to develop a sense of belonging and confidence in the couple's commitment to an ongoing relationship

■ to erect boundaries which permit both the development of an intimate relationship separate from the families of origin and the growth of the two individuals within the relationship. This is one reason why it is often wise to postpone the birth of the first baby until the couple has become consolidated.

■ to provide sufficient nurture for trust and growth.

Moving on

Infants grow by becoming more mobile and co-ordinated, moving away from mother, at first for short periods, and then for longer until eventually they can go to playgroup, then school and finally gain independence. Similarly, this stage of a relationship cannot last, however much we might want it to. Mirroring a baby's first steps, one or both partners will evince signs of outside interests: maybe relationships with former friends will be revived, or the exigencies of a job will take priority. The first baby may arrive with all its demands on the mother's time and energy. The intimate glow of romance fades fast in the chilly light of a 5a.m. feed. Differences, which hitherto the couple may have unconsciously colluded in keeping hidden—often at the expense of part of their true selves—become apparent, then more marked. The couple are then at the crossroads, and must start down the bumpy track of accepting their differentness, and seeing that it can enhance rather then mar their relationship.

Beth and Bryan

Beth and Bryan separated after three months of marriage. They had met when Beth had just discovered she was pregnant and was panicking about the prospect of having a baby on her own. Her parents were unwilling to have her at home, and she felt lost and abandoned. Bryan took her in, let her live in his flat, cared for her, and fell in love with her, enveloping her with his feelings of warmth and tenderness. In her gratitude and need she responded, and they agreed to marry a few months after the birth of the baby.

During the time of waiting their relationship looked like a fairy tale, and they lived for each other. Once the baby was born Beth realized she could cope with both life and motherhood, and had grave doubts about marrying Bryan. She saw clearly that, although she valued what he had done for her, he had a strong need to be needed and had a weak personality. She went, leaving him feeling abandoned and rubbished, mourning the relationship, her absence and the baby with whom he had bonded. Their idyll had ended abruptly.

In those few intimate months, Beth had grown from a frightened child into a mature woman, and Bryan had provided the nurture which had enabled this growth. Bryan had grown up feeling unneeded, being one of seven children and born soon after a stillbirth which his mother mourned for years. Counselling helped him understand his need to be needed and his sense of loss, and enabled him to express these. It took time, but he came also to see that Beth had given him something—the knowledge that he was lovable and desirable.

The transition from romance to reality is one of the most difficult the couple has to bridge, for it is often characterized by disappointment and disillusion. Frequently one partner is more ready and more willing to move forward than the other, with all the turbulence that this will inevitably bring about in a young relationship. When one partner wants to do something separate or different, this can provoke pain, anger, tears... and rows may result. The pain is all the more acute if the partner who seeks to prolong the security of the first stage has scarcely separated emotionally from their family of origin and still craves love and attention, for they will feel stranded and unsupported.

The greater the need for nurture and love (and if it was lacking in infancy the need will be overpowering), the more intense will be this time in a relationship. An extreme example of the 'transference' phenomenon (a feeling towards a figure earlier in life transferred onto a current significant other) is shown in the desperation of one man in the early months of his marriage. His mother had given him away for adoption in the first weeks of his life, changed her mind, taken him back, then rejected him again. When he married, he pleaded for hours to be spent with him in bed, and cried to his new wife: 'Sometimes I think I could just climb back into your womb and stay there for ever.'

Greater also will be the pressure of the needy partner on the other to keep on providing cosseting and mothering. The psychological immaturity of someone whose needs belong to an earlier stage of personal development, and who is insatiable for reassurance, can erode a relationship. Erich Fromm describes the process:

> *Greed is a bottomless pit which exhausts the person in an endless effort to satisfy the need without ever reaching satisfaction...* [the person] *is always restless, always driven by the fear of not getting enough, of missing something, of being deprived of something.*[22]

One of the strongest unconscious purposes of falling in love and marrying is to find once more the unconditional love and acceptance of infancy. But that is the fantasy of the romance stage; infancy never comes again. If we try and force our mate to act as a parent, the marriage will suffer. People who cling desperately to fantasy will eventually erode the relationship.

Attempts to prolong the exclusivity and symbiotic nature of the early days of the relationship can also result in controlling, even cruel behaviour, which can include addictions, jealousy, frequent illness and exaggerated dependency:

> *'Have you looked in the mirror lately?' he asked as his wife was packing her bags. 'You're not as beautiful as you were when we got married. Sometimes I can see the stubble on your legs. And you wear make-up now. You never used to. Sometimes, you put on so much you look like a clown! Who'll have you if you leave me?'*[23]

Frankie and Bob

Frankie and Bob formed a relationship when they took their children to the local skating rink twice a week. They decided that Frankie would leave her partner and Bob his wife. But Bob was unable to accept that Frankie was really committed to him, and was prey to a destructive jealousy. He couldn't even call Frankie's previous partner by his name, but always referred to him as 'the printer'.

Frankie had truly finished with her former partner, but Bob insisted she give up her job at the dentist's in case 'the printer' came as a patient. Everything they argued about focused on 'the printer', who assumed an obsessive importance in Bob's desire to keep Frankie exclusively his 'property'.

Sue and Barry

Sue and Barry had met at a disco when she was fifteen and he seventeen. Barry's mother had just died. He had never known his father and had been in care. He also had a record of juvenile crime. Sue had not had much parental attention or affection, and couldn't believe that Barry wanted to be with her. Barry, in turn, had at once fallen for Sue, saying she was beautiful and wonderful and would turn any head. He idolized her from that moment, and what appealed to him was her 'freedom'.

They married two years later but, ironically, Barry's obsessive behaviour turned this 'free' but still needy child into an imprisoned woman, who was not allowed to go anywhere, do anything, but who accepted the situation because of her own low self-esteem.

When, one night fifteen years later, Sue came home at two in the morning, Barry was convinced she was having an affair. He acted the private detective, going to extreme lengths to find out the name and address of his suspect, whom he hounded using scare tactics. His self-doubt erupted in violence on his wife, and he found himself out of control.

Such behaviours are obviously counterproductive. Nevertheless, we are all human and often our own worst enemies. Certainly, total sacrifice is beyond us, according to American author and teacher, John Powell:

> *Theoretically, I believe that if a person could continue offering an unconditional love, the other would in time respond. But perhaps the response would come too late. If the person trying to offer unconditional love is given nothing in response, to nourish the capacity and renew the strength for love, the relationship may be brought to an inevitable failure.*[24]

Getting stuck

> *Their daily life seems uncommonly intimate. Rising early to strains of classical music, one of them feeds the horses before a joint breakfast... lunch à deux, more work before a ride together, then a cosy dinner and an early bed... True to form, they seem almost uncomfortable with the brief parting necessitated by Terence having to locate their hotel bedroom while Charlotte goes on to the restaurant. Until his return, her conversation is halting, becoming relaxed only after he has taken his seat.*
>
> *Such rapport is mystical... a matter of finding your other half in a blaze of recognition... The only problem with such closeness and mutual support is that it can make life hard for outsiders, even children. 'Both children elected to go to boarding school,' Charlotte agrees. 'They wanted to get away from that constant intimacy—the sight of the two of us locked in a room; it meant they never saw either of us alone.'*[25]

This striking example of a couple entrenched in the 'romance' stage is not an excerpt from the pages of a Mills and Boon romance, but a description from an article in the *Daily Telegraph* in 1995 of the real-life, 32-year-old marriage of romantic novelist Charlotte Bingham and Terence Brady, who, it would seem, have succeeded in keeping their idyll for nearly a third of a century. In many couples, this unwillingness to cope without each other might be a sign of being stuck in, or too terrified to move out of, this stage.

Here is another 30-year-old marriage:

Husband: *We enjoy doing everything together, be it playing Scrabble or Pick Up Sticks—doing things together rather than sitting reading a book or doing other things or watching TV.*

Wife: *The way he expresses anger is to go and do something on his own.*

Family therapists use the words 'enmeshed', 'merged', or 'undifferentiated' for the state of getting stuck in this first phase of life together. The characteristics of these couples are:

- an emphasis on 'we' rather than 'I';

- clinging of one partner (or both);

- high anxiety about being abandoned;

- inability to see each other as separate;

- emotional 'submerging' of one partner by the other;

- emotional blackmail if there is any suspicion of 'differentness'.

At this level of emotional immaturity, attempts at negotiation or solving problems will be met with hysteria and panic.

The couple who spent the first year or so of their marriage alone on a boat continued to do everything together, even when land-based. Even several years into marriage they tended not to have separate friends, and presented a solid front to all their social network. They had, in fact, cohabited for some years before their marriage and although the wife, Yvonne, said that this helped her maintain an artificial sense of independence, she reluctantly acknowledged her very real emotional dependence once married.

Both men and women will often go to great lengths to try to imprison their spouses in this romantic other world. To do so they will attempt to exert extremes of control, and their partners will often collude because of their own emotional hunger and need for dependence—until the balance shifts. The following is a story of what is known as a 'doll's house marriage' (after Ibsen's play, *The Doll's House*, which describes a fragile, dependent, childlike wife and her controlling husband, and how the dynamic of their marriage changes to reveal him as the needy one).

Listen to Mary's story. A shy, young girl from a small town, she was taken in by a strict aunt after both of her parents died. Mary learned early to keep her mouth shut and do as she was told. Always a poor student, she lacked confidence in her own intelligence and never considered continuing her education after high school. Around men, Mary kept her eyes lowered and her voice soft. She married young and depended on her husband for everything. Very often, he didn't provide it...

As soon as her kids were in school all day, Mary got a job. 'It changed my life,' she says. 'I met lots of people. They liked me. They told me jokes, and I remembered them and began telling them to other people. And they laughed. I mean, they thought I was a scream. Me! I liked work so much, I started dressing up for it. I had my hair colored. I wore mascara. People told me I was pretty. The manager gave me a raise. So I decided to go back to school. And it turned out I really was smart. I got good grades! I used to run to the bus in the morning, that's how eager I was to get to work. Soon I got up the courage to leave my husband. Now I have an apartment of my own and friends of my own and a nice boyfriend who'—she blushes at this— 'makes me very happy. I am a completely independent person who doesn't lean on anyone, and it's all because of my fabulous job!'

What 'fabulous job' changed Mary's life? She was a check-out operator at a supermarket.[26]

Being unwilling to move on from the exclusive, dependent/controlling stage may make it into a prison from which the only way of escape is to break out—separation or divorce. But it is possible to move on rather than out, if conflict is recognized as a signal for growth. The choice, as ever, is ours.

CHAPTER 7

Reality

'THAT'S IT FOR THE WARM-UP'

Sooner or later most recently-married couples will wake up in the cold light of reality, and discover that their relationship is not a perpetual state of being in love, 'oneness', and having sex and fun. The harsh facts of living together break in on their idyll. Passion can dissolve into ordinariness, aided by the fatigue and stress of balancing home and work. The first hint that romance is fading is often the realization of differentness, and it may take the form of the accusation, 'You've changed! You're not the person I married any more!'

Husband: I think obviously some of the magic wears down, and there's also disillusion. I guess some traps snap shut; with others the door closes slowly and you're inside the cage.

Wife: I think the real change came once Michael was sure I was committed. Once he felt he had me trapped it was much different to beforehand.

This couple, both in their second marriage, were describing what they both felt after they had been together for just over a year. In it we can hear bitterness, hurt and disappointment at the change in what had started out as a passionate, intense and whirlwind romance.

For some couples, this realization can produce difficult times. Fault-finding, blame, a row—or rows—may follow, accentuating the newly perceived distance between the individuals. At the same time, the responsibilities and problems of daily living become more challenging: one partner may forget to pay a vital bill; there is dirty washing left on the floor; weary home-comings in the evening after work prohibit romantic meals and inhibit sexual performance. Pregnancy can be exhausting, and the early days of parenthood can put huge strains on a couple both physically, emotionally and often materially as well.

If the ecstasy doesn't last we can feel bitter and disappointed, and if we cannot communicate this, and our needs, then there will be a lot of pitfalls in front of us as romance wears thin and the relationship is ready to move on:

You speak like a young man, and a young man that is in love... This is mere rhapsody; it will vanish in an instant before the reality of life.

Benjamin Disraeli, *Coningsby*

Expectations

The higher and more unrealistic our expectations of wedded life, the harder we shall fall. These expectations of the roles of husband and wife are largely derived from our childhood when we observed our parents and the roles they had within the relationship. We are also formed by the way they handled their own 'differentness', their differences and conflict, how well they communicated, and what the 'rules' were in our family of origin.

Tricia and Gavin

Tricia's parents had an extremely traditional marriage, and were in their forties when she—their only child—was born. Father left the house at 8a.m. to commute to work, and returned at 7.15p.m. to his supper ready and his slippers warming. He was the provider, while his wife depended on him for everything. Tricia's father actually referred to the relationship as being a contract—'I will be the breadwinner, and you will run the household.' In her own marriage Tricia expected provision to be made, not so much for material things (as she had her own job), but for all her emotional needs, for she was highly dependent. Her husband, Gavin, brought up in a wartime family where father was absent, had no model of a husband taking care of his wife. Bitter conflict resulted between these two immature people, which was never resolved satisfactorily.

Roles which worked well for our parents may be inappropriate for us. For one thing, we are not our parents; for another we come to our marriage with (usually) a set of parents each, and the models they have set before us may be scarcely compatible. Again, social changes bring different conceptions of marriage. Dr Jack Dominian, the psychiatrist and guru of marriage, writing about the proposals for divorce law reform in *The Independent* of 27 April 1995, said:

> *The high divorce rate is due to many factors, but prominent among them is the changing nature of marriage from a contract of social roles, where the husband was the breadwinner and the wife mother and homemaker, to an egalitarian relationship of love. The latter requires social skills of communication, availability, affirmation and resolution of conflict.*

Separating ourselves emotionally and physically from our family of origin when we marry also means distancing ourselves from its patterns of behaviour and interaction in order to forge our own relationship, one which is appropriate to us as a couple. This requires the communication of our needs and wants, hopes and expectations, and the recognition and the abandonment—or at least renegotiation—of those which are unrealistic and not conducive to the progress of our life together.

Balancing home and work

The worlds of home and work cannot be totally separate, for to a large extent they are interdependent. The stress and strain of work can easily spill over into the home environment, and so also can our domestic problems affect performance and relationships at work. As much as dramatic crises, it is the ordinary everyday reality of becoming and living as a couple that causes the stress to take its toll. Similarly, it is the daily work situation which will make its mark on the household. Thus a central focus of learning to accept the reality of coupledom is to get the right balance between the demands of a job and the needs of the spouse and family. Both marriage and work are part of our total life experience, and they interact and affect our performance, efficiency and satisfaction.

Accurate communication between the couple about their own needs and expectations, and how these can be integrated with the exigencies of earning a living, must be part of this phase.

The role of conflict

However hard it is, however much we may want to cling, to be dependent and to control, the relationship has to begin to grow up and mature. And this, as with infant and mother, means an increasing ability to be separate. The couple, or one partner, may try hard to sustain their 'togetherness' and avoid disagreement, but ultimately a prolonged avoidance of conflict will lead to a static and stagnating relationship, for we shall neither truly know nor accept the reality of our partner or ourselves. Differences and conflict can be steps to growth.

Sally and John

Sally and John met at a party where drugs were freely used. They were both regular users, though Sally managed (just) to hold down a job. Both had come from families where there had been quite severe emotional deprivation. They married a few months later, and Sally fell pregnant almost immediately. She took drugs all the way through her pregnancy, and although she coped with the early days of motherhood, once the baby became mobile she couldn't manage as she was almost always stoned. Realizing the impossibility of the situation, she had her son put into care. This triggered off a desire in both partners to stop doing drugs, because in their lucid moments they realized they didn't know each other at all, and had no idea whether their relationship had any firm basis. There was a long haul ahead before they could finally sever themselves from drugs. When they did, they realized they were strangers to each other. This was reality with a vengeance—the sober light of day breaking in on what had been a drugged fantasy.

Sally's incentive was to get back her child, and this helped her keep off drugs. She had to learn first of all to accept and love herself, before she could accept and love John, or care for a young child, so it was the reality of herself she had to confront first. Gradually she was able to tell John that she didn't like his irresponsibility and refusal to work, and what her own needs were from the marriage.

Through this genuine communication between them, John was enabled to change sufficiently to take more responsibility, and eventually he became a mature student and found a good job. This in turn gave him the self-esteem which he had lacked in childhood, having always been in the shadow of a brilliant younger brother. They both kept off drugs, managed to hold down jobs, and their child was returned home to them.

The 'jumble bag' scenario

Enter a couple—Jack and Jill. Each is carrying a smart leather case in one hand and a plastic bin liner in another. For a long moment they embrace passionately. When they come out of their clinch, they sit down beside each other and admire each other's smart case. Jack explains that his case contains all the wonderful things he has to give Jill during their life together. Jill replies that her case contains everything she wants to share with Jack. One by one the objects in the smart cases are brought out and shown to the other, who gazes rapturously at them and at the beloved. This is what they get out of their cases:

Jack	Jill
• all my love	• all my love
• my gentleness	• my tenderness
• my strength	• my motherliness
• my savings	• my body
• my religion	• my smile
• my sexiness	• my privacy
• my name	• my toothpaste
• my love of football	• my teddy bears
• my CDs	• my good cooking

After this exchange the couple continue to look longingly and lovingly at each other. Then they catch sight of the shabby bin liners they are carrying. Slowly they bring out the contents of these jumble bags:

Jack	Jill
• my laziness	• my untidiness
• my dislike of foreign food	• my temper
• my awful relatives	• my sad memories
• my smelly socks	• my scatty friends
• my unshaven face	• my nagging
• my prejudices	• my extravagance with money
• my angry memories	• my obsession with my weight
• my snoring	• my unpunctuality
• my insecurity	• my hours on the telephone
• an old toy train	• an old tattered dolly

At this second stage of marriage, the partners each encounter what the other has been hiding in the 'jumble bag'. Some of the hidden side of the other may elicit compassion, understanding and sympathy, but some will be the cause of irritation, recrimination and even bitterness, for in the blindness of love we often believe we know the whole person—only to have the scales removed from our eyes by the nitty-gritty of daily living. When the couple bring out the last item in their jumble bag— the old toy—it is an admission that there are times when we all behave more like children than adults, and that we too still have tantrums and tears as well as a need for play and fun. If the couple are secure in their love, and if the first stage of their relationship has achieved a sense of trust and belonging, they will be able to accept more easily that each individual is a complex mixture of personality—positive and negative. This stage means accommodating all these different facets. It can also mean adapting to the fact that the qualities which were most endearing earlier can be those which cause stress and conflict now.

The 'shadow side' emerges

The truth is, of course, that neither we nor our partner have changed; it is merely that we are getting to know them. In the language we used in Chapter 2, the 'shadow side' is emerging. This is a good sign, however difficult it may be to come to terms with. When we start encountering blocks in the relationship, niggles and disappointments, then this is the signal that we have something to learn both about the other and about ourselves:

Helen: It was total disillusionment.

Michael: Well, we got on, but we certainly had some lows, and we learned more about each other than we wanted to know.

But in this life, and certainly in intimate relationship, there is no gain without pain. We are hurt when people do not live up to the expectations we have created of them, and it is hard to renounce the fantasy that in our spouse and lover we had found the knight in shining armour (or indeed the sex goddess with a PhD) who could fulfil all our needs and dreams. In our immaturity, we marry so our partner can 'make' us happy. We depend on the other to provide for us emotionally, as a parent provides all for the child.

Couples who sought to complete themselves in each other are, as we have seen, those whose relationship with their own parents was lacking and unsatisfactory, and who have failed to resolve this 'unfinished business'. These men and women will not be free, yet, to build a new relationship with their partners which is based on reality and the freedom to be themselves, nor to appreciate the other as they truly are.

If letting go of fantasy is hard, it is even harder to learn that in reality we are responsible for the fulfilment of our own needs. In our frustration and out fury we project our pain: '*you* are hurting me; *you* are making me unhappy; *you* have changed'. And the partner who is the recipient of all this can unconsciously collude by taking on board this load of guilt, believing themselves to be responsible for the resulting pain.

Getting stuck

Marriages stuck at this stage are characterized by one partner trying to coerce the other to come back into the former state of blissful oneness.

As we saw in the last chapter, they may beg, plead and threaten in ways which only serve to drive the other further away. The other may initially try to go along with this—to help the one who cannot bear aloneness, or maybe just for a quiet life. But anger and resentment will eventually well up, causing conflict, and the merest suggestion that the clinging partner might also like to go out on their own may provoke insecurity. This can be a time of great stress and strife, which can often be prolonged for many years.

James and Christine

James had been married for twenty-five years when he spoke for the first time of his domestic problems. He admitted that when he married Christine, he was immature and knew little about relationships. When they had first met, each sought in the other the affection which had been lacking in their early lives, but they were too needy to give it. Over the years, Christine became a sporadic heavy drinker, abusive and violent when drunk, subjecting him to vicious and humiliating verbal attacks. She was also a heavy smoker, (about sixty a day), which was now, at age forty-six, badly affecting her health. Often James would come home to find her lying unconscious in her vomit. When she came to, she would turn to him and demand sex, which he felt unable to provide.

James carried round a heavy burden of guilt for many years, believing he had failed Christine. There are, of course, many factors active in addiction, but Christine was saying, in effect, 'You are responsible for my welfare and my well-being. You are responsible for my anger and disappointment with life. Until you make me happy I shall go on slowly killing myself—and it will be your fault.' But Christine would not talk about her needs or about how things could be improved, nor see a doctor or psychiatrist, and she refused to take steps to become free of her addictions.

This is an example of the emotional blackmail of a dependent partner, who will go to extreme and counter-productive lengths to prolong the exclusive possession of the spouse. Ill health of one sort or another can also be a typically controlling behaviour, which is an attempt to keep the spouse close.

This time of getting to grips with the reality of our partner coincides with a period when the young relationship appears at sixes and sevens. Husband and wife may not come to a realization at the same time that they do not have to do everything together, or feel the same way at the same time, and if this is the case one of them may feel even further rejected and let down.

The tasks of Stage 2

The tasks of this stage are among the most difficult that a couple will encounter:

■ Husband and wife must start to accept that they cannot rely on each other to fulfil all their needs in the way a mother intuits and meets the needs of her baby.

■ They must work out new patterns of relating to each other. They must allow themselves and their partner time apart, away from each other. To this end, they must re-establish contacts with friends and family as well as continuing to enjoy activities together.

■ Their differing expectations of each other and of the roles of husband and wife must be acknowledged and reconciled. This means seeing each other as equal adults and not as parent or child. To do this each must learn to acknowledge and communicate their needs.

■ They must learn to compromise, redesigning their personal goals and responsibilities as adults.

■ As children arrive, the couple must work out together and balance the multiple roles of wife/husband; mother/father; care/provider.

■ The rules of the relationship, as well as its structure, must be hammered out. The couple must learn ways of dealing with tension and conflict while staying close and connected.

Moving on

When both partners have achieved these tasks well enough they will move on towards the next stage. This will happen when they can recognize and affirm each other's differentness and individuality, and when their expectations of each other and of the relationship become realistic. This second stage of marriage mirrors the time in childhood when a baby begins to realize it is separate from mother, understanding that there are times when she doesn't provide for every need on demand and when it can physically begin to move away from her, albeit for short periods.

CHAPTER 8

Power Struggles

'A RESISTANCE WORKOUT'

There are plenty of reasons to hope that in marriage, differences and rows can bring greater awareness of both ourselves and the other and so lead us further on along the road of relationship. As Richardson's *Grandison* has it:

> *The falling out of Lovers is the renewal of Love. Are we not now better friends than if we had never differed?*

We must hang on to this hope as we enter the third phase of marriage, for conflict can be a constant at this time, leading to pain and break-up, and a situation of cold—or active—war.

A few years into the marriage the interests of both partners will be diverging and developing independently, and there is usually far less will on either side to accommodate and compromise. At this stage of their journey, the couple can *feel* distant and unconnected, and they will often be pitted against each other in a battle of wills to see who has control. It is now obvious that our spouse is very different from the person we thought we married. Accusations are now made with less worry about the effect they have.

Chris and Ursula

Chris and Ursula had been married for nine years. He was a social worker and she a news photographer, and their children, aged eight and seven, went to the local primary school. Huge storms blew up whenever one of the children was too ill to go to school. Chris insisted that his job was of more value than Ursula's, since it brought in slightly more money and was in a 'caring' profession. Ursula, who had returned to work two years before, argued that she had to build up her career, needed to be available at short notice, and that no newspaper would give her work if she was unreliable. The rows were long and bitter, and the children suffered—often being sent to school when they should have been in bed, whereupon both the parents would race each other to avoid the inevitable telephone calls from the school authorities requesting them to come and fetch whichever child was ill.

In the case of Chris and Ursula, the couple were locked in a power struggle where each was more scared of giving way, and thus of losing their own identity, than of the consequences of these embattled scenarios. Giving way appeared to mean handing over the power in the relationship, and losing too much of themselves.

At this stage, complaints and disagreements may abound; the disputes are more open, less inhibited. What is mirrored is the battle of the toddler with mother. 'No! Shan't!' is the response of the young child fighting out the question, 'Who decides?', and a similar tussle is taking place in the marriage. It has been said that our struggle with our partner grows out of the battles of the parent and child 'still smouldering within our own psyches', the script for which was written within our individual nurseries.[27] If our childhood issues of independence and power were not resolved then, we shall replay the scenarios until they are.

The child... actively searches for autonomy and more opportunities to exercise his own choice... Since the central issue is one of control, the encounter between the child and his mother is always a contest, and often a head-on collision.[28]

Polarizations, patterns and projections

Joe: It wasn't that I disagreed with you booking the holiday in France. It just wasn't my first choice; I made that quite clear. But you have edited that out of your memory.

Maggie: But you couldn't come up with a better suggestion, could you, and we had to get on and book something.

Joe: But there was another suggestion.

Maggie: This was a self-catering in Portugal. The way I remember it was that you didn't like the idea of self-catering. I thought you'd vetoed that idea.

Joe: No I hadn't. I thought that was what you were going to do, because there were things for the children to do there.

Maggie: I thought you'd vetoed Portugal.

Joe: No I hadn't, but I just didn't want to go camping in France, but if that's what you must have, I suppose we'll have to do it...

Maggie: It's amazing how you remember things differently.

The specific trigger for these conflicts—the peg on which the argument is hung—will vary in each case. It could be, as above, a seemingly specific matter of where to go on holiday, or how to handle sex, money, leisure, children, in-laws or any one of a hundred domestic concerns. But whatever it is, a certain pattern of external conflict seems common to couples at this stage. One of the major distinguishing features of this era in the marriage is that the partners tend to polarize their roles: parent/child; bad-tempered/martyred; dominant/submissive; self-indulgent/self-denying; saver/spendthrift, and so on. In the course of their struggles, one partner will usually act as the disappointed one (the blamer), while the other will be the one who is held responsible. Those who blame the most are often insecure, vulnerable and deprived people who have little trust in the other's desire to stay with them or to love or help them.

'Continued blame is the communication of despair,' says Christopher Clulow, chairman of the Tavistock Institute of Marital Studies, and this despair often dates from childhood. Those of us who perpetually blame others are often those who live in the painful paradox of finding intimacy and trust difficult, but who are also terrified of separateness and aloneness.

As we saw in Chapter 2, the hidden traits of the married couple emerge during the course of the relationship. We may have been attracted in the first place by the very opposite of the feature on which the attraction is unconsciously based. In the 'doll's house marriage', the insecure young women seeks a competent and dominant man, but in fact selects a partner in whom these attributes are covering up a desire for security similar to her own. A similar phenomenon is the subject of Scott Fitzgerald's *Tender is the Night*.

This polarization of roles and characteristics during the couple's interaction will reveal the unconscious elements which once drew them together but which now account for the often intractable nature of the struggle which is going on between them. If couples can understand what is happening to them, what these unconscious aspects of themselves and of the other are, then this stage can offer one of the best and strongest exercises for change and growth. If, on the other hand, they get entrenched in their rows the relationship will slide down into a sort of bitter immobility.

We can recognize in each other the disowned parts of ourselves, for these are often the very opposite aspects of our own obvious characteristics. The dominant partner may be projecting their own unconscious fear of dependence onto the spouse to enhance their shaky self-esteem, while the dominated partner may be allowing the other spouse to take control of certain areas which they do not feel able to cope with. The partner of the excessively prudish person may be carrying the other's fear of sexuality. The confusion and fighting of this stage are often attempts to integrate the contradicting parts, and blame and recrimination may reflect an individual's own inner conflict.

As rows continue and the spouses diverge, they will become progressively distant and disengaged emotionally. Compromise demands too much surrender of our individual identities, and the more insecure we are, the less we shall actually possess of our self in order to give way or say sorry.

Thus the relationship suffers, and we arrive at a place where we no longer support each other in the quest for growth and independence. If this is the case, chaos reigns within the relationship, and this is often the time when partners might first seek emotional and, or, physical solace outside the marriage in someone who appears less belligerent and more understanding.

The bedroom as theatre of war

Sex is one of the couple's primary modes of communication; it is the ultimate in body language. It can thus be seen as a barometer of the couple's relationship outside the bedroom. If they are in the phase of trying to control each other, of gaining the power within the relationship, then the marriage bed can become a gladiatorial arena.

Those stuck in the power struggle stage and who seek to control their partners are often those who have not moved emotionally beyond the 'anal phase' described in Chapter 4. These 'controllers' are rarely adequate sexually as they are unable to let go—a feature of intimate and satisfactory sex. Similarly, people who have deep-down fears of being left may experience little desire for sexual intimacy because of the inevitability of bodily separation that follows it. As Christopher Clulow puts it in *Marriage Inside Out*,

At an unconscious level, distaste, lack of desire or avoidance of bodily intimacy may be used as a defence against the experience of ultimate aloneness which can follow the fusion of intercourse... Similarly, those who cannot bear to know about [their differentness] *out of bed, and whose marriage is based more on identification than complementarity, can be disturbed by actual bodily differences which cannot be ignored in bed.*

'No! Shan't!'—the refusal of one's body, or the forcing of it on the other—is the ultimate in control and emotional victory over the other. Sex can all too often be about power struggle.

The tasks of Stage 3

■ to develop a sense of our own power and be able to share this with our partner—rather than try and control them

■ to bring the hidden aspects of both partners into view and to enlarge the boundaries of the relationship in order to accommodate these

■ to reconcile the polarizations which have now become evident, and to begin to accept both the positive and negative facets of ourselves and our partner

■ to work out our own unresolved power issues from childhood without dominating the other

■ to develop problem-solving, decision-making and negotiating procedures within the relationship so that in dialogue we do not crush each other

■ to work at maintaining enough love, connectedness, and awareness of each other's needs and feelings while this is going on.

Getting stuck

If the tasks are not worked at then a couple can stick in this phase for years, even decades, for patterns observed from their parents will be deeply ingrained. The cat-and-dog marriage frequently runs from generation to generation, and is characterized by stinging exchanges, rather than dialogue, with accusations which begin:

'You always... '

'You never... '

'Why can't you ever... '

'Be back on time or else... '

'Stop nagging... '

'I'll please myself... '

... ending up with one or the other flouncing or stomping from the room.

Conflict flares up rapidly, and couples stuck in this stage feel the need to assert themselves vehemently. However, sulking and silences can be equally powerful means of controlling a situation *à deux*. This exchange took place in front of a researcher:

David: We both go into a real huff, and we don't talk to each other. I mean last night we had one. We didn't speak or hug before we went to sleep. We were in a huff.

Yvonne: We had a difficult telephone conversation with my sister.

David: She's being a wally.

Yvonne: No she's not.

David: That's a guaranteed wind-up because Yvonne won't accept her family are a bunch of f...... wallies. We're both real sulkers, we put our pride on the line. But my pride is less tender than yours.

Yvonne: What!

David: I normally come and give you a hug first.

Yvonne: No, you don't. If I know I'm right I'll give you a hug first.

David: I'm very fast—I resent strongly and quickly, and I won't say a word to her. Often there is no resolution. You bury it, you don't resolve it. It has to do with the fundamental way we are. It recurs—over and over and over again until we die. Either you live with it or you opt out.

Yvonne: Or you negotiate.

David: There's no negotiation over those things. You can't negotiate over fundamental, irrevocable, unchangeable facets of being. That's it.

If young children never resolve their power struggle with their parents, if they are not given the firm boundaries and limits which—although fought against—bring security within which to grow, then for the rest of their lives insecurity will cause them to push against any limitation on their power or authority unless the pattern can be broken in adult relationship.

It is a painful time if this power struggle is prolonged and intense, and positions of accusation and blame become entrenched.

Moving on

It is at this stage that couples most often benefit from outside and objective help in order to be able to move out of and away from these polarized positions. They will be able to progress once more if they can both:

♥ recognize their need to control

♥ take steps to reconnect by

   ● talking more

   ● making an effort to understand the other's perspective

   ● acknowledging what the other partner is feeling ('I know you're feeling let down, but... ')

♥ see patterns of entrenchment which come from unresolved struggles with parents.

When this can be done, husband and wife are on the way to relinquishing their power struggles in favour of co-operation and greater intimacy.

Gerry and Felicity

The story of Gerry and Felicity shows that sometimes it is necessary to retrace our steps back to an earlier stage of the marriage journey. Gerry had grown up in a family where he had always felt second best and devalued. His older brother was adored by his mother and could do no wrong. When Gerald married Felicity, life was good: here at last was a woman who didn't make him feel small. For ten years they were apparently happy, but then things started to go less well, and Felicity, a teacher, confessed she had had an affair with a colleague.

Immediately Gerry retaliated by saying that he too had had an affair a year before. From then on there was war. They were two hurt and bitter people who could not stop blaming each other, recriminating and accusing. Neither could admit the needs that had driven them, but continually accused the other. Everything now became ammunition in their struggle. There were constant rows, and at one point Gerry left home but was dragged back by the children. He now felt once again as he had felt long ago—second best. He became depressed, drank too much and his standards of dress and hygiene slumped.

In counselling, Gerry came to understand the root of his feelings of being second best, and for the first time he spoke of his lack of self-worth. Felicity revealed how guilty she felt about the way she had brought up the children, and her own lack of self-esteem. She also was able to tell Gerry, in the safety of the counselling room, that she had turned down her former lover's invitation to go away with him, and had broken off the affair. In time, Gerry came to understand that in fact he was not second best in their relationship, and he learnt to appreciate Felicity's needs. He gradually ceased his 'oral' gratification of drinking too much, and grew up. Their sex-life resumed, and their marriage went back to start its 'romance' phase all over again, this time with more solid foundations of communication and dialogue.

Who Am I?

'QUITE A DELIBERATE STEP'

According to a recent newspaper article, if those who grew up before the Swinging Sixties missed out on a liberated youth, they seem to be embracing it now. They are putting themselves first in their later years, filling universities and colleges of further education, setting off—as Shirley Valentine did—on foreign adventures and, increasingly, consulting marriage counsellors about how to cope with their spouses.[25]

This can also happen to people in their forties or thirties, echoing the adolescent struggling to answer the question, 'Who am I?' Teenagers will often search for the answer by distancing themselves from their parents and their values, frequently doing so physically by moving away from the family home. It is a time of discovery which precedes what psychobabble tends to call 'self-actualization' and autonomy from parents. So it is in marriage, for this phase mirrors that of the adolescent identity crisis. For marriage partners, this part of the journey all too often coincides with similar crises in their teenage children, and the cumulative effect of all this can make for a time of tension within the home. It is natural for offspring in their late teens to leave home; but for a spouse to do so can signal the end of the marriage.

These are the middle years and they are often fraught with change and stress both from outside and from within. There is recognition, especially by men, that they have gone as far as they are going with their career; yet their wives, who may have not long returned to full-time employment, may just be relishing a new job. There may be early retirement or redundancy; there may be elderly parents who, at the end of their own lives, need care; there may be teenagers who create havoc, or adult children who sometimes return to make inquiries about their early years or to make peace with their parents. In the midst of all this, husband and wife can experience—consciously or unconsciously—a mounting pressure to resolve their own unfinished business of the past. The death of our own parents is an event which should never be underestimated in its power to provoke what is popularly called a mid-life crisis.

The Swiss psychologist, Carl Jung, theorized that in every significant relationship there is one partner who is the 'container' and one who is 'contained'. The container provides the stability, and the other the spontaneity and vitality; one may provide the framework of competence for the practicalities of married life (finance, DIY, home-making, or childcare), while the other brings colour and variety. Together they complement each other and make a whole—married people often speak of their 'other half'. During a marriage the emphasis can shift slightly between one and the other, but generally one partner will display more 'container' attributes and the other more of the 'contained'.

During these middle years, however, a crossover sometimes occurs. As we traverse the rocky patch from immature dependence to greater autonomy, making our way towards emotional maturity, this stage in the journey can bring crisis and change. If the couple can negotiate the changeover the experience will be enriching. If not, it can diminish them or even provoke the breakdown of the relationship. Here is one husband, in a job which required frequent moving, whose marriage was enhanced by his wife's new independence and sense of self:

Jack: She saw herself as camp follower. We went all over the place and she just followed without any question. Then she trained as a social worker... discovered she had an enormously important role in her own right, and so she developed that, and learned and studied, and it was really then that she began to discover her gifts, and over a period

*of time grew much faster than I did, and that's been
quite fun. I've observed many marriages where people
have grown at different paces and resent each other
when the other's growing, but actually it's been very
creative.*

These are the years when responsibility patterns can change,
especially in 'traditional' families where the wife has remained
in the home to bring up the children: now she is free to develop
her own personality and interests, become her own self, and
gain new confidence. Many men can be threatened by this, and
it can mean a loss in the amount of 'mothering' they too
receive. A confident and more assertive woman may find that
just as her children have outgrown the family home, so she has
outgrown the need for what marriage can give her in terms of
safety and security.

It is also worth remembering that at this and every stage we all
regress when under stress. Teenagers (as we saw in Chapter 3) can
revert to being infantile, and in adult life the effect of difficulties in
the home may well be to turn us, however momentarily, into big
screaming babies.

*As time went by, all Lucy could think about was the many
differences between them. He was twelve years older, which
meant, among other things, that he was thinking ahead to
retirement when she was still looking forward to a career.
He'd gone to university; she hadn't. He didn't get her jokes;
she didn't appreciate his. He worried about money; she
was a spendthrift... As the years wore on, Tom and Lucy
seemed to occupy parallel universes. 'The communication
wasn't what it should have been,' Tom admits. 'It was like
a one-way dialogue. I couldn't tell where she was coming
from.' And then, with increasing regularity, there were
arguments.*

*Finally, in the last year, relations closed down almost
entirely. Tom had the distinct impression that Lucy was
trying to push him out of the house. Lucy says she simply
withdrew from him. She started taking walks around a*

nearby lake, where she met Edward who, even though he was nearly sixty, seemed to offer much of what Tom did not.

John Sedgwick

This portrait of a recently-divorced couple shows them moving from Stage 3 of their journey (power struggle) to the breakdown of their relationship. Instead of being able to keep open their dialogue, instead of accepting their differences and using them as a rich resource, they—or at least the wife—looked elsewhere for new interest, a renewed sense of esteem, for completion of the self. Perhaps if they had known better how to communicate with each other, if they had sought help over how to do so, they would have understood that their quest to integrate their 'shadow side' or 'hidden self' was as yet incomplete and that their differentness offered a step to growth. Lucy might have perceived and explored certain recurrent patterns in her life, one of which was her attraction to older men.

An affair or a new permanent relationship will usually serve only to switch the focus, and can be a diversion from the real issue of finding and completing one's true self. Nevertheless there are therapists who have been known to say that an affair can revitalize a marriage, and we will look in more detail at the extra-marital relationship later in this chapter. The impulse to run away from the marriage can be strong at this time, and discontent is heard in the all-too-natural cry of 'I want time for myself'; 'I want some space'; 'I've brought up the children, I've always been there; it's my turn now!' And sometimes it will be necessary for the couple to withdraw from each other emotionally and, or, physically in order to find out, who they are individually and what they want (see 'A trial separation', later in this chapter).

The word 'fulfilment' often figures during this stage, and our own needs become paramount, sometimes driving us to seek their satisfaction outside a marriage which, if the previous stages have not been satisfactorily resolved, can seem empty or painful. Certainly, if a strong basis of trust has not been established earlier, the relationship can deteriorate disastrously now. Unless we understand that no relationship can ever, of itself, fulfil *all* our needs, the chasm between partners can widen to a point which will be bridgeable only with huge effort, and talk of separation or divorce may now feature seriously in the couple's exchanges. This can, of course, often be a ploy to control and bring the 'erring' partner back into the relationship.

Counselling

Quite often counselling or therapy is sought now. It is undeniably true that the future of the marriage may depend largely on whether the counsellor treats the relationship as 'the client', or, conversely, sees only the individual spouse that seeks help as the one whose needs are to be addressed. Counselling can indeed be about 'finding out who we are', about recognizing our resources and capitalizing on them, as well as understanding the factors which lead us to behave the way we do. Through outside help (objectively in counselling or subjectively in a liaison with another) the partner whose self-esteem is low can find strength, confidence, and the spur to grow. However, sensitive counselling of the *relationship* (which may also involve individual sessions), for those committed to their marriage vows, can help husband and wife to discover their real selves *and* integrate this richness into the relationship. At the same time it can teach them the skills of listening, reflecting back what the other has said, and recognizing and communicating their real feelings rather than a litany of blame and complaint.

Even if the couple do not actually go their separate ways at this point in their journey, they must become separate individuals, just as adolescents must separate from their family and childhood home. The transference phenomenon can be strong here—we can unconsciously view our partner as the parent who is trying to stifle our growth towards independence, and our progress will depend on the tightrope walk between expressing our own 'adolescent' emotional vulnerability and our need to become 'ourselves', and hanging on to this fragile sense of self-identity in the midst of all that is going on in our lives. Therein lies another paradox of married life: in both the adolescent-parent relationship and the marriage at this stage, the former issues of nurture, power and independence evolve into a struggle to maintain intimacy between increasingly separate individuals.

Having an affair

An affair can occur at almost any stage in the journey of marriage except in the early romantic days. In the days when we are getting to grips with the reality of our relationship and partner, the affair can be a desperate bid of one spouse to experience a sense of worth and importance, to feel an excitement that they sense is waning at home. It may be an attempt at emotional blackmail of the other partner: 'If you don't show me you love me I'll get what I want elsewhere.' It can, in Stage 3 of the marriage, be a means of asserting independence or wielding power over our partner. In Stage 4 it may be an attempt to discover our true self, for it is certain that most people can find out who they are only in a close relationship with another.

But an extra-marital fling, or even a more serious relationship, is not likely to help us disclose our 'shadow' side, or to resolve personal issues from the past, for—because of its clandestine, stop-go intensity—it will prolong the fantasy-inducing, psychological blindness experienced by lovers in the 'romance' phase. However, on the plus side, it can provide much-needed self-esteem and worth which the deceived partner does not, cannot or will not give. Jack Dominian often quotes the archetypal husband seen in therapy who says, when his wife complains of feeling unloved:

'I told you I loved you twenty-five years ago. Why do you need me to say it again?'

An affair, in giving our confidence a much-needed boost and making us aware of qualities not drawn out by our spouse, can thus sometimes be the spur to the self-discovery which will lead us away from the marriage and into a more independent way of living. But all too often, however, it is a new way of making an old mistake (like the man we saw in Chapter 2, whose mistress was a carbon copy of his wife).

Nevertheless, an affair, especially at this time during a marriage, need not necessarily sound the death knell of the relationship between husband and wife, but can actually strengthen it if both are willing to work hard at getting to know themselves and each other better, and at looking at what hangovers from childhood relationships are preventing them from relating intimately to each other. 'Forgiving and forgetting' will not of themselves work, for it is unlikely that the 'betrayed' spouse will be able to renew trust after infidelity as though nothing had happened. If the reasons for the affair are not excavated and examined, then true forgiveness (which involves understanding as well as compassion and trust) cannot exist.

Affairs rarely appear out of the blue, though they may come as a surprise both to the partner involved, and—when the secret is out—to the other. Usually there has been some level of dissatisfaction on one or both sides for quite a while, but the couple do not know how to communicate these feelings or how to handle the difficulties which arise from their struggles for power or independence. Here is a (male) marriage counsellor talking:

> *There is certainly a big change going on out there, especially in terms of women and what they're looking for in relationship, and what they're willing to put up with, and she* [the current client] *seems to me to reflect that. She's now in her mid-forties and is at a point where life isn't OK any more, and hasn't been for a long time. The way she describes it is, 'My emotional needs are not being met and haven't been for a long while, and it's not OK.' Her husband has no idea of what she means.*

> *When she married she wanted a secure, stable, rock-like figure to provide what she'd never had as a child. And he did, and that was OK for a time. She was very dependent on him at the beginning. But she started to move on and he didn't, so the relationship itself didn't move. She had moaned for years, but this time it was different. It wasn't going to go away; she was ripe for a really good affair; she*

wanted an exciting guy. If she'd been able to kick up this fuss ten years ago it might have worked, but he's sort of solidified. He won't, can't, move on.

For those whose emotional development was arrested by being deprived of affection and tenderness, the need to be the centre of someone's life and the overwhelming desire for love (or the illusion of it) can drive us to indiscretion and folly. A thirst for excitement and fantasy will lure us on, sometimes into a string of affairs, with common elements, which are abandoned when reality breaks in or the same patterns repeat. And if our family of origin did not know how to express anger or if early scars left us fearing intimacy then we are more susceptible to the pull of a relationship which, by its very nature, will not be able to address issues which require a deep foundation of knowledge and trust.

Liberty Kovacs, the American family and marital therapist, says:

Another factor that's very important is who abandoned this person in the first place. Almost invariably, I find that the partner who had the affair was abandoned—literally or emotionally—by a parent or someone close to them when they were children. Psychologically, they may be re-enacting the same scene as adults, except they become the one who abandons. It's a subconscious feeling they have to re-enact the situation in order to resolve it.[29]

There are other—more circumstantial—issues involved when it comes to affairs: increased opportunity and plenty of cash give British males in social classes 1 and 2 the edge on their working class brothers. As suggested by preliminary results released in January 1995 from the Wellcome survey on sex in the UK, the 'bosses' are five times more likely to have had more than one sexual partner in the past five years than the 'workers' (those in classes 4 and 5).

Christina Hardyment comments in the *Daily Telegraph* of 1 April 1995:

There is also the consideration that the gender difference in extra-marital sexual activity mirrors exactly the moment when women wave children off to boarding school or university and set themselves firmly in the saddle of a full-time career. By then, men may well have realised that their chosen profession has careered just about as far as it will go and they seek consolation in the mini-skirted young hopeful who has just turned up in Accounts.

And for many women, too, there is something undeniably sexy about an affluent or powerful or well-known man which may somehow be tied in with their own efforts to resolve issues of power and independence.

Rebuilding trust

This must begin with the partner who had the affair committing themselves anew to the marriage and to being faithful to it, and perforce making the decision never to see the lover again. Trust will not be rebuilt overnight, and if a separation has occurred it may well be that a time of reflection away from each other may produce better results than immediately getting back together, with all the resultant tension and opportunities for recrimination. A separation can induce a fruitful regression to the pre-marriage or honeymoon stage for a while—with the couple ringing each other, arranging meetings and outings, trying a day or two alone together, attempting to recapture some of the excitement and romance of their early days. However hard it is to exclude children who may have been hurt, frightened and traumatized by rows and rupture, at this instant some moments of exclusive 'togetherness' must be built into the agenda.

To help themselves understand what has been going on in the marriage so that blame and remorse—the great killers of relationship—can be diminished, the couple may need counselling, some of which may include sex therapy or counselling, in order to reinject excitement and discovery into a sex life which may long since have 'gone off the boil'. All this will demand a high level of commitment and hard work. The 'betrayed' partner may need a great deal of reassurance and nurturing—going back to Stage 1—in order to regain trust.

Building up a relationship again after an affair, with all the painful issues of trust and fidelity to be renegotiated, is a long and difficult process—a leg of the journey which requires much effort. The partner who has had the affair, even though 'back' in the marriage and committed to it, may grieve the loss of the lover and the former relationship, and the other partner will have to deal with the pain and sense of betrayal, and then let go of these consciously in order to rebuild the partnership.

A trial separation

If a couple are having difficulty in dealing with their need for independence, and conflict is prolonged and bitter, and if they have reached a stage where they cannot be objective about their relationship yet wish nonetheless to save their marriage, then they can benefit from a trial separation. This will usually be the case when they have grown disengaged and distant to the point where they have difficulty understanding each other's needs, sometimes when an affair has been discovered or 'revealed'. Sometimes the separation will be *de facto*, for one will have moved out—back to the parental home or to a friend. If the separation just 'happens' in anger and despair, and its structure and guidelines are not agreed by the couple, then any return to the marital home is likely to renew the old patterns; trust will not be re-established despite good intentions, and communication will never be improved.

A structured trial separation can provide a much-needed breathing space in which partners can gain a more realistic view of the relationship, and gauge whether they miss each other sufficiently to return to the relationship out of a sense of belonging rather than from guilt or duty. They should at this point discuss their personal fears about whether the relationship will or will not ever be viable again. It may be that a separation now is the first time in their lives that one or both will have lived alone; it is their first chance to become self-reliant, independent and competent, to reflect on their lives, the recurring patterns within the relationship (and to take responsibility for them rather than blaming their spouse), and to develop their own interests in order to become more fully the person they have the potential to be.

A trial separation can avoid the trauma of those couples who divorce only to find they wish to remarry each other. This is the story of Viv Burgess who divorced her husband Geoff on the grounds of his adultery in 1989 after thirteen years of marriage. They remarried in 1994:

> *So I divorced him. After that, I would see him every weekend when he came back to see Michael. I was doing my degree and starting to enjoy being independent. I think he started to respect me more than when I was just a housewife bringing up a child. Divorcing was the best thing that could have happened because it made him realize what he wanted.*
> *Daily Telegraph*, 17 November 1994

For a trial separation to serve its purpose the following elements need to be discussed by the couple:

♥ **Living arrangements**: merely dividing the family home into two separate living quarters will not work, nor will a temporary move into a friend's house, for the husband and wife need to experience 'aloneness' and to explore their reaction to it. Only this can give them the time and space to develop their interests without feeling selfish.

♥ **Children**: the children need to be told considerately that their parents are going to live apart for a while and for how long, and that this is a way of trying to make the marriage work rather than a necessary forerunner to divorce. Children should be given the opportunity to voice their own feelings and anxieties—it could be that their parents take it in turns to live out in rented accommodation so as not to disrupt the children. It can often happen that the parent in charge of the children finds the relationship with them closer and more real, for the bickering and bitterness of conjugal life is no longer sapping their energy and distracting them.

♥ **Money**: all the implications and practicalities of running two households concurrently for a while must be thoroughly discussed and settled before any separation.

♥ **Length of separation**: the minimum period of transition from being a couple back to being single again is around three months, which is sufficient space to miss the other person and to assess the repair and rebuilding work which needs to be done in the relationship.

♥ **Personal contact** between the couple: this needs careful negotiation, as does the question of whether husband and wife will consider themselves free to go out with members of the opposite sex during this period. A full-blown relationship at this time would, as we have just seen, remove the focus from the individual and relationship issues that the separation is designed to highlight and help resolve. The couple must decide for themselves on the frequency of their meetings and stick to what they have agreed. If they are having counselling they will of course see each other there; otherwise, neutral territory is safer. Later on during the period of separation they can arrange meetings and outings, and can talk on the telephone—as at the beginning of a relationship.

♥ **Sex**: if they are in counselling together, this is the place to debate the re-establishment of sexual activity. If they have used their time apart to grow as people and know themselves better, then they will be more open to a discussion of past problems and of their needs and wants. Sexual contact and satisfaction can now be seen as the natural extension of the conscious efforts they are making, in planning meetings and activities together, to do things together that are pleasurable, fun and which will provide 'glue' to the relationship.

Even if no major crisis blows up during this part of the journey, even if husband and wife stay together—travelling forwards though perhaps not so close together as once they were—the fitness of their marriage needs constant care and attention, especially during the years when there is so much to distract and fatigue, in order that the partners can find a measure of self-knowledge which will enable them to be independent and intimate at the same time.

The tasks of Stage 4

■ to make a conscious choice in favour of the relationship as a way of life

■ to achieve separateness and independence

■ to discover and hold on to our own identity

■ to see and appreciate our partner as a separate person

■ to be able to express more emotional vulncrability within the relationship

■ to improve negotiation skills, and to learn new and better ways of conflict resolution.

Moving on

If these tasks are completed, the husband and wife will

♥ be able to recognize, accept and learn to live with their own and the other's strengths and limitations;

♥ be able to make sense of and find consistency in their separateness and maintain their individuality within the relationship, resolving issues of independence together rather than outside the marriage;

♥ be well on the way to the next stage.

The equipment they will need to do all this is the ability to make their needs and wants known to the other in a way which is neither threatening nor pleading.

CHAPTER 10

Working It Through

'MORE SMOOTHLY AND WITH CONTROL'

If man and wife have come this far along their journey together through marriage, they will have a clear and confident idea of who they are as individuals and how they can and do relate to each other. But many couples will not have made it this distance, for their own individual emotional development and lack of resolution of early issues will weigh them down too much to develop further as a couple. To have got to this stage they will have developed their communication skills and learned much about conflict resolution, problem solving and negotiation in order to fulfil their needs and achieve their wants. Here is one couple after twenty-nine years of stable and happy marriage talking about how they arrive at marital harmony.

Question: Do you generally agree with each other?

Wife: Usually; we do usually.

Husband: It depends on how we phrase the question. You have to ask the right questions to get the right answers, don't you? We know how to ask each other the right questions.

It will have taken the couple half a lifetime of time and energy, commitment and constancy to have arrived at this sense of love and respect for each other's individuality, at an enjoyment of being able to broach any issue that comes up. They now feel safe in pursuing interests separately, yet enjoy being together when not doing so. The couple quoted above were obliged to be apart from Monday to Friday and were able to cope well with this separation because they now possessed themselves fully as people. At weekends they were able to fit easily back into a more intimate life together. A marriage at this stage has to be flexible enough to include two individuals and the relationship itself, and it also has to be accepting and tolerant of the strengths and weaknesses of each.

The desire for independence now is recognized as a quest for continued growth rather than a rejection or an abandonment, for each possesses a full identity which is self-sufficient, though willingly shared. The man and wife collaborate more easily in the tasks of daily living and decision-making. They will take responsibility for their own feelings, needs, wants and ideas, and thus the relationship will be based much more firmly on a clear view of reality:

> *The most compelling measure of* [mental] *health seems to be the degree to which you face reality; that is, the degree to which you perceive it, and accept it. Then, parallel with that, there's the extent to which you behave inclusively— that is, try to include other people, new ideas, and your own perceptions and feelings, rather than exclude them. But I suspect that's really just an aspect of facing reality— which is, after all, inclusive!* [30]

Because they are secure in each other, the couple will confront differences and potential conflict much earlier on, for disagreement or anger will not be the end of the world nor will they cause the diminishment of either person:

> **Husband:** *We have done so much together, discussed and worked. We can discuss things and work together, and come up with a compromise which we can both accept without either of us always giving in.*

> **Wife:** *And we can have some pretty hectic rows and make up and neither of us bears grudges.*

Another couple, married for thirty-five years, announced only half-jokingly that—taking their cue from French parking regulations—one of them would agree to be in the wrong on even dates, the other on odd ones. They said it worked.

Unresolved conflicts

Openness, honesty, genuineness and respect for the other lead to much deeper emotional closeness, because we are not hiding our real selves or protecting our insecurities, and it is along this path that the couple make their way during this phase of their marriage. Nevertheless, unresolved conflicts from the family of origin are still likely to make their presence felt.

Andrew and Georgina

Andrew and Georgina had enjoyed a rich and fulfilling marriage and had recently celebrated their silver wedding. Their two daughters had left home, and one had married in the past year. Andrew planned early retirement, and both were looking forward to this phase of their life together and to spending increased time with each other as well as pursuing their own many and varied interests. Andrew duly retired at fifty-five, and Georgina's reaction took them both by surprise:

Georgina: I felt crowded, I felt threatened, I was irritable and I raged at the least thing. It wasn't just that I missed my space and the independence I had grown used to; it was much more profound than that. I couldn't cope.

Georgina saw a counsellor, for she was frightened that what was a stable marriage was being eroded by her constant feeling of threat, and that she and Andrew were not enjoying his retirement as they had expected. With the tension came a return to the 'power struggles' phase, and even further back to the second leg of the journey where she discovered that she barely knew the reality of the person she had married. With the help of her counsellor, Georgina was able to perceive a direct parallel between her feelings of threat and invasion when the father she didn't know had returned from the war when she was four.

She was reliving all her old unresolved feelings and transferring them onto this new interloper in her home— her husband. Once these feelings were acknowledged, it became easier to deal with them and talk to Andrew about them, who in turn learned much more about his wife's needs and expectations. The tension in their household eased. Their story demonstrates the need to go back and do particular tasks again, sometimes more than once.

This period can be marked by just such a recognition of our own past conflicts and the effect they bring to bear on the people we are now. Part of this acceptance of the self means understanding that there will always be parts of ourselves which have unreasonable expectations of the other. Equally, it demands a recognition that neither our partner nor we ourselves will live up to the expectations we have.

The tasks of Stage 5

■ once again consciously to choose this relationship as a way of life

■ to achieve a clear sense of our 'self' and that of the other

■ to take responsibility for our own feelings, thoughts and behaviour

■ to share the practical responsibilities of daily life

■ to support each other's strengths and successes

■ to progress from independence to interdependence. This involves maintaining our sense of individuality while working towards intimacy.

Moving on

This budding interdependence (rather than dependence on the other for our needs, or an independence which separates us from our partner and prohibits intimacy) is the step to the final stage. The couple who are moving forward at this time will be characterized by:

♥ the use of disagreement and conflict as an opportunity to learn about themselves

♥ confronting conflict earlier, and handling it through negotiation

♥ expressing anger without it being a threat to the relationship or the other person

♥ being able to state wants and needs openly and easily

♥ maintaining individual identity within the relationship

♥ communicating more directly

♥ increased collaboration

♥ consideration of the other's needs and wants

♥ a firm grounding in reality

♥ a high level of warmth, love and intimacy.

When all this forms the basis of the relationship, the couple will be near to perhaps the richest and most rewarding part of their life together, one that requires less effort from them just to keep going forward—thus liberating their energy for renewed creativity and enjoyment of life.

However, they must learn to recognize and accept that they will often have to go back and retrace their steps when the need arises. Crisis and trauma from outside the marriage, or illness of one of the partners, will cause us to regress to an earlier stage of our personal development; our need to be dependent, cared for and nurtured will then increase. These regressions can be either traps to fall into, or steps to growth—the impetus to an increased knowledge of each other and ourselves. Which way these challenges will take us will test our ability as a couple to communicate and negotiate.

CHAPTER 11

Collaboration

'TIME TO RELAX'

The man and the woman who, in their personal development, have reached a point where they have acquired self-esteem and self-appreciation, will probably have become interdependent in their relationship. They will see themselves and their partner as they truly are, and will enjoy being both together and apart.

> *My own self must be as much an object of my love as another person. The affirmation of one's own life, happiness, growth, freedom is rooted in one's capacity to live, i.e. in care, respect, responsibility and knowledge. If an individual is able to love productively, he loves himself too.*[31]

Here are one couple, Stephen and Sarah, whose journey has brought them to a relationship of interdependence, describing their marriage of twenty-eight years:

> *Stephen: I think there is actually a mixture of closeness and distance, because in spite of the fact that I think we describe ourselves as being close when we're close together, we also provide each other with a licence to be away doing their own thing.*

> *Sarah: I think it underlines the good relationship and understanding—and the knowledge that one of us will 'hold' the other when things are stressful. We don't necessarily stand any nonsense but the one will 'hold' the other.*

The process of arriving at this stage is complex and demonstrates the link between personal and marital development. The marriage has contributed security and self-knowledge to the personal itinerary; but the marriage would not have got to this point if the two partners had not achieved the necessary degree of emotional maturity. John Powell describes this cycle:

> *You will look into my eyes and see there the great cause for self-celebration and I shall see my beauty, my value in your eyes. I want to be the first of the invited guests at your celebration-of-self party. And I want you to come to my party; because without you there never could have been such a party. When there is unity like this... happiness cannot be far away.*[31]

This is the stage of the marriage journey where we have already struggled up many hills together, where we may at times have taken divergent paths, but now we look forward in a spirit of collaboration. Collaboration takes for granted that we are committed to each other, that we share each other's joys and help carry each other's burdens: the two individuals have become two 'I's' making up a 'we'; yet within this they still retain a clear sense of the autonomous 'I'.

Here Stephen and Sarah are discussing what their daughters will take into their own marriages from that of their parents:

Stephen: They've seen too many of their friends' parents where harmony is far from the norm. But they will know it is possible.

Sarah: I think they will take the possibility of that as a model. Yes. Harmony with freedom. Basic harmony. With Andrea and Joanna it's very strong that they will value their independence but that that will be all right. That independence can work.

Stephen: I think that's probably one of the most difficult things for them to appreciate at first: that you can actually be a couple but be independent.

Sarah: Separate but together.

Stephen: Mmmm... They've seen people who've been separate, but they haven't seen too many people who are that and together, and have within certain brackets their independence... or interdependence.

At this time in a marriage the husband and wife meet challenges together, sometimes succeeding, sometimes failing. They have a sense of togetherness, of unity and collaboration. One close couple, married for twenty-six years, faced personal catastrophe when the wife went into hospital for tests where she was diagnosed as having motor neurone disease, while the husband was in another hospital some miles away with surgeons fighting to save his right arm.

They both said afterwards that they could cope with their future; the really hard part was going through the anxiety of tests and surgery apart and unable to communicate with each other, except by a coin phone wheeled round the wards of their respective hospitals.

Collaboration brings with it increased sharing and intimacy. Although this may be a time of life when the menopause may pose difficulties for some women, many older couples find that their sexual life is a powerful symbol (and means of expression) of the stage which their life together has reached, as these interviews show:

Lovemaking gets better the closer you are to someone; for a start you don't have to worry about holding your stomach in.

Any improvements in sensation are lovely and subtle, and there's something sweet about an 'old married couple' coupling like a cosy pair of bears.

Being totally relaxed with your partner means you can really let go and the tension released is greater as a result.

I tend to treat making love as something precious to be worked at.

John Sedgwick

At this stage, the couple have already started to handle problems, conflicts or difficulties much sooner after they crop up, for they are secure enough in themselves and in their relationship no longer to be afraid of anger, and they know how to negotiate. Because the couple feel fully accepting and accepted the relationship flows naturally, and neither has to worry about trying to please, impress or placate the other. This certainty gives them a secure base from which to look outward, to fulfil themselves without having to invest all their energy—emotional and physical—in keeping together a relationship, at the same time as balancing the demands of children, household and career. This energy can release a great spurt of personal growth, for in many ways we have come full circle back to the unconditional acceptance of infancy, which is the starting point of all growth. But this time it is mutual and reciprocated, fully aware.

Again, because of the security they have, a couple can, without losing anything of themselves, go backwards and forwards along the road they have travelled—collecting, in the words of one counsellor, 'bonuses of love and romance and memories on the way'.

Is it all rosy glow at last? Have they found what they were looking for in the blissful days of romance? It is certain that where they are now looks very different from where they started out, and although they would not deny the journey has been tough—'I've been married for forty years and I don't know how we've done it' (marriage counselling tutor)—most would say that the view now is infinitely better, for it is a clear view of reality. This stage will not be without problems, those that are common to ageing (elderly parents, adult children's problems, illness, retirement, reduced income and failing ability) but the couple who have come to this part of the journey will have the emotional resources to cope. One of the effects of crisis, as we saw in the previous chapter, will be to send them back through some of the earlier stages of their relationship.

The tasks of Stage 6

The tasks of this stage are much the same as those for the previous one, but in addition ageing must be tackled, which means:

- accepting graciously and gratefully the help from other sources which becomes necessary as age increases;

- learning to live on retirement income;

- preparing for the approaching and inevitable end of our own lives by building or strengthening values and beliefs by which we can live—and die—in peace.

At a conference in 1992 about changing trends in contemporary marriage, the psychologist Paul Brown suggested that this declaration on the nature of the lifelong encounter between husband and wife should be enshrined as the basis of law:

We hold it as self-evident that through their differences, men and women create a unity and a wholeness which is for the great benefit of themselves as individuals, the nation and the future of the human race. We therefore enshrine in this declaration their interdependent equality as well as recognize their differences...

This brings us full circle to the initial definition of marriage as something both intensely private but which has a public dimension. The couple who have journeyed through a lifetime together will have the confidence and the freedom to look outward beyond themselves.

Postscript to Part II

Our image throughout this book has been of marriage as a journey for which the couple have to be emotionally and psychologically fit, and in which they will not be able to see, let alone move on to, the next leg until they have satisfactorily completed their current one. This mirrors our own personal path through life—emotional, psycho-sexual, moral, cognitive and spiritual—in terms of stages. One theory of personal development postulates that it is our needs which are the primary influences on our behaviour, determining our motivations and priorities, and governing our actions.[32] We have already seen some of the ways in which the unrequited needs of early childhood will affect our intimate relationships—as babies we may scream and yell for gratification, tenderness and comfort; in adult relationships this behaviour can be destructive and self-defeating, but we will continue to behave in this way, often in ever more inappropriate scenarios, unless we find someone to break the pattern and hold us securely.

Our levels of need are many and diverse: physical, emotional, social, intellectual and spiritual; and, just as in the journey of marriage, we must be secure in the first step in order to proceed to the next. The non-fulfilment of our basic needs (survival; safety; security; to be appreciated and accepted within the relationship) creates immature, locked-in behaviour patterns, which will go on repeating until the need is met. Once it is, however, then an individual (or a relationship, or a society) will be motivated and liberated to go on to the 'higher' needs (for respect and self-respect, achievement; 'self-actualization'—realizing one's potential), finally to know and understand and tackle the unknown.

A major study of 373 couples by Professor Elizabeth Douvan[33] found that what is called 'affective affirmation', in other words the verbal and physical communication of love, is so powerful in marriage that it brings about a remarkable transformation. The unconditional approval of our mate can actually move us closer to being the ideal that they seek. Douvan says:

If he is accepted for the way he is, he winds up doing things her way. And she moves towards his way.

What are the implications for the married couple, and indeed for any relationship?

First, we must each become aware of our own needs and of those of the other. To know what our own needs are we must learn to listen to our feelings. How do I *really* feel:

♥ when you read the newspaper instead of talking to me when you come home?

♥ when you turn over and fall asleep immediately after we've made love?

♥ when you spend an hour and a half on the phone to your mother?

♥ when you forget my birthday?

♥ when you forget to pay the phone bill and we're cut off?

♥ when you drink too much when we're at a party with friends?

♥ when you smell of someone else's scent/aftershave?

When we have analysed our real emotions (often masked by anger) we may be more in touch with our feelings. These will reveal the extent of our needs. Next we must communicate these needs accurately and without blame or accusation to our partner, so they can understand our need and have a better chance of meeting it. The communication of our deep-down feelings, with the vulnerability that this demands, will do much to defuse situations of conflict or stalemate.

PART III
'Good Enough' Marriages

CHAPTER 12

Cross-training

CONFLICT: CAUSES, MANAGEMENT, COUNSELLING, DIVORCE

Edna and Dave

Edna (aged fifty-three) was starting the second year of a degree course which took her away from home quite often. Recently she had told her husband Dave (also fifty-three) about a brief affair she had had with a man at the college. Desperate rows ensued, and the couple went to a marriage counsellor. During counselling it became clear that Edna's new-found self-confidence was disturbing Dave, and he was becoming anxious and depressed. Edna tried to convince him that she loved him, but he wanted her to end her studies, and she refused. The quarrels became bitter.

After several sessions, the counsellor helped them to agree a compromise with Dave starting a business enterprise scheme. Edna was enabled to understand for the first time Dave's deep-seated fear of losing her and to link this with the divorce of his parents when he was young. They ended counselling with encouraging prospects for both, and a relationship which was more mutual.

In any intimate relationship conflict is not only inevitable but it is necessary. Couples who claim always to have lived in sweet and unalloyed harmony (and there are those who say they do) are deceiving themselves, or they are avoiding or suppressing important issues. Conflict shows us that our relationship is alive, and that we are ready to move on and grow; and if we can hang on to the fact that tension is, or can be, a transition point, it can help us to deal with it. It has been said that 'the only good conflict is a resolved conflict', but this chapter will suggest that the *process* of resolution is often more important than the end result.

We have seen that it is vital that a couple's eyes be opened to the fact that they are different, that they see clearly in the other what truly belongs to them and what has been the projection of the self onto the beloved. If these differences are not perceived and integrated into the relationship, it cannot advance. Accepting the truth that our partner is not as we once believed in the first blindness of love is often a painful and bitter process, fraught with opportunities for discord. Later, as we have seen, the struggle for control and power (whose needs will dominate?) within the relationship, and then the distancing which occurs when the husband and wife struggle to discover and come to terms with who they really are, will provide ample cause for conflict.

> *She was married to this chewing, frowning fat man. She was married to him. A craziness rose in her... the sense of her unregarded self coming painfully to life like a numbed extremity. As so often, this formed itself in a kind of anger.*
>
> *'You might talk to me. We don't often get any time to ourselves.'*
>
> *'What about? I'm not used to talking. It's been a bad day.'*
>
> *'I know. But we never talk.'*
>
> *'Can I have some more vegetables?'*
>
> *... She had meant to say something loving, from her to him. Who was he? What did he care about? He was a good, a practical man. She loved him. Did she not?*
>
> *'I don't understand'... He gestured...*
>
> A.S. Byatt, *Still Life*

His reality and her reality

It does not take us long, once past puberty, to grasp the fundamental and underlying fact that men and women are not merely different physically, but emotionally, psychologically and probably mentally as well. It is no good railing 'Why can't a woman be more like a man?'—she is not. Neither is any male, even the New Man, capable of reacting entirely as a woman does. Recent research at the University of Pennsylvania has suggested that gender differences in handling emotions are related to differences in male and female brains: men are better at tasks requiring dexterity, and women at some verbal tasks and those requiring emotional judgment. Men tend to express emotion by action; women tend to put it into words.

When men and women both say they want 'togetherness' in marriage they mean different things. Women tend to want close companionship, but men seek a pleasant base for their lives. Already, therefore, in our expectations of marriage there is the seed of discord. This fundamental dichotomy in our perspectives of the universe cannot be eradicated, but it can be modified by men and women staying open and listening to each other's reality.

We handle conflict in radically different ways, too, which can, if not understood, erode the relationship. Because men have more difficulty in putting emotion into words they will flee; but women will fight. Furthermore, other research[34] shows that men react more strongly physiologically than women during marital conflict, or even in the anticipation of it.

Add our gender conditioning as children to our genetic programming—women are conditioned to seek their psychological satisfaction through the provision of support for the activities of others; men are encouraged to provide concrete and visible contributions—and here is a potent mixture for bickering. Translated into terms of moral developmental stages, many women will not go beyond Kohlberg's stage 3 and will attempt to get their own needs met by making others happy (see Chapter 4). If they feel dissatisfied enough, they may transpose this outside the marriage. The man tends to be more sexually oriented than the woman, who is more interested in the relationship's emotional context. Furthermore, their perception or memory of the same event, or their interpretation of the same words, may well differ.

In other words, when men and women talk about their marriage, there is always his reality and her reality.

In a marriage it is frequently the wife who, more tuned in to what is called 'emotional literacy', seizes the chance for growth and struggles towards maturity, while the husband is all too content for things to stay the way they are. It is more frequently the needs of the wife which change radically through the years of marriage.

Counsellor: He was a stable, inflexible, unchanging sort of guy. It took quite some time for him to realize she was serious about her needs. He kept saying, 'I wish I could wake up and all this stuff about her needs would have gone away'. I think he knows now that if he doesn't do something this marriage is going to come apart, so now he's willing to try; he's desperate for it to continue. But it's not a positive reason for change. I think it did work at the beginning, it did fit. He was the stable, rock-like figure to her little girl, but when it all blew up a while ago it was because she'd taken a job for the first time, and he allowed her to do it providing everything went on at home exactly the same. The arguments started because he had her in a particular role, but her emotional needs took her away from that.

Conflict in an intimate relationship

Conflict between two people in intimate relationship occurs when there is a difference, disagreement or an incompatibility; and the closer the relationship the more fertile the ground for conflict. However, the course that the conflict will take will depend heavily on where the individuals are in their personal development. Taken to an extreme, it can mean that someone who is still emotionally a thwarted toddler can lash out violently with words—or blows. We can grow from conflict more easily when we can trust the other with our emotions, when we are beyond the stage of 'who decides?', and when we have a secure sense of our own identity.

In the early stages of marriage, especially when the dawn of reality is breaking and the couple are adjusting to the everyday nitty-gritty of life together, conflict will take the form of specific disagreements, an argument over a particular issue. It may be a difference of opinion or view, a complaint, criticism, a hostile or coercive response from one or the other, defensive behaviour or an action which displeases. These can lead to an overt disagreement.

In the stormy years where man and wife may be engaged in a struggle for power and independence, trying to carve out their own identity from the rockface of marriage, their relationship can become severely dysfunctional through conflict, unless they have negotiated the early years well. Conflict will cause unhappiness which they may be powerless to resolve without help, and the relationship may gradually dissolve.

If, however, the couple communicate well at more than a superficial level, and have a solid and secure basis of love, then conflict will take more the form of a problem-solving discussion, where they use negotiation and bargaining skills. The subject of these discussions is more likely to be an ongoing issue rather than a one-off issue of conflict. This will tend to typify couples in the final two stages of their journey, but more recently married partners can acquire and use these skills.

Paul and Liz

Paul, a self-employed electrician of thirty-two, was referred for counselling by his doctor. He came with his wife, Liz, who was clearly irritated with him and told the counsellor how she spent most of her time alone with their two small children. He was totally preoccupied with his work and was becoming exhausted and depressed. Their sexual relationship was almost non-existent. They could no longer talk without quarrelling. Paul explained that his first duty was to provide a good home and all the comforts for his family, and so he worked all the hours God sent. He noticed how Liz had stopped telling him about her days, and he became suspicious that she was seeing another man. He couldn't discuss this with her because she became angry and dismissive.

Over some weeks the counsellor helped them discuss their fears and misunderstandings in a way they could not manage when they were alone. Paul started to reorganize his work to spend more time at home, and stopped believing that Liz would be unfaithful to him. Both learned to relax with each other and to be more loving.

Defence mechanisms

In close relationship we are by definition vulnerable; our real self emerges. When times are good we are trusting enough to let our partner see this in confidence, but in times of conflict we feel naked and defenceless, for in revealing part of our true identity we have given deadly ammunition to our partner to use against us. So even in intimacy we tend to use the defence mechanisms that are necessary for our survival in the wider world and that are now (because we began to shield ourselves with them so young) an integral part of our personality. In conflict we shall run for cover behind them. This can be a problem in a relationship, for it takes up energy to keep hiding. Because these mechanisms also falsify, distort and deny reality, we cannot grow as individuals or as part of a relationship at the times when we are too busy clutching fig-leaves over our emotional private parts; but these are the times when it is arguably most important that we grow.

The most commonly used defence mechanism is one we have spoken of earlier: projection. We transfer onto our partner a characteristic or feeling in ourselves with which we are not comfortable or happy.

Marcia and Robin

Marcia, whose father had been a stickler for punctuality, order and discipline, greatly feared her own 'sloppiness' as her father had called it. Because she was afraid of being late she made strenuous efforts always to be on time, and in consequence tended to spend unnecessary hours of her life waiting at airports or on station platforms, always urged on by the inner voice which forbade her to be late. She married Robin, who was laid-back and relaxed about timing, and projected onto him her own unacknowledged laziness, of which she was so afraid. As a result of this projection, and in the first whirlwind of being in love, she ran happily to their assignations without needing to make any effort. A few months into marriage, however, Robin's bad time-keeping irritated her more and more, and Marcia's inner voice became a reality, projected not at herself but onto her husband, nagging Robin to be on time and jump to it. This inner conflict of Marcia's was deflected onto Robin, and the initial attraction of his relaxed attitude soon brought her into real conflict with him.

Other means by which we defend our emotional nakedness are:

♥ **denial**—we refuse absolutely to own one of our characteristics, often accusing our partner of having them instead

♥ **repression**—we block out from our consciousness all that causes us pain or fear, in terms of behaviour, events or emotions

♥ **displacement**—the husband and wife whose marriage is deeply painful and who have come to despise each other may row quite violently about trivial matters to avoid the real issue. Another example might involve being hauled over the coals at work and then not daring to speak our mind back to the boss; instead we come home and give our spouse or children—or the cat— absolute hell. Conversely, our hatred of someone close, which feels too dangerous to acknowledge, can be transposed into violent reactions elsewhere—for example, at the driving wheel, or at the football match

♥ **identification**—in our desire to be lovable we select and adopt those qualities in others that we think will help us achieve our desired goal. Young people model themselves on sports personalities or rock stars; insecure parents may feel they have always disappointed their own parents and may in turn put enormous pressure onto their own children to succeed, finding it unbearable if they do not get brilliant exam marks, or if they should lose a job. Some people may even require their pets to be of impeccable pedigree, so they can somehow identify with their flawless good looks!

♥ **rationalization**—we find acceptable reasons for our own behaviour, to the point of being dishonest with ourselves. How often do we say, 'I can't go without a chocolate bar/a drink in the morning, because... ', when what we really mean is 'I *don't* go without it'? Or, 'I can't stick with my marriage without having an affair.'

♥ **reaction formation**—this is the exaggeration or overcompensation of certain conscious traits of character or behaviour, as a defence against opposite, unconscious ones that we fear are unacceptable. The person who has stopped drinking or smoking may moralize priggishly about those who still indulge, from a fear that he or she has not really kicked the habit. We may be highly pedantic in, say, our use of English if unconsciously we have huge doubts about our linguistic ability. Or we may be extremely sensitive and emotional, to mask what we fear is an uncaring, selfish personality

♥ **regression**—we have seen how under stress we often try to escape back to an earlier stage of our development which feels safer, and where we are under less pressure to cope with reality by ourselves. In a desire for nurture we may be physically ill; we may go to pieces so we can be looked after and shed our responsibilities; we may turn to compulsive addictive behaviours in a desire for consolation (comfort eating or perhaps the bottle).

If a relationship becomes threatening for any reason, we all take flight in a conflict situation and hide behind some of these defences to a greater or lesser degree. To resolve conflict, however, we have to bring our real selves out into the light of truth, and accept the risk of pain that this vulnerability brings.

Areas of conflict

Any couple at any stage of their journey can enter into a conflict situation, but it is axiomatic that dissatisfied couples will squabble more readily for less cause. However, for couples at all stages the following areas can be problematic:

- ♥ **Communication**—spending time together, conversations, sharing feelings, recreation and lifestyle.

- ♥ **Sex**—physical affection, including manner, style and frequency of intercourse.

- ♥ **Jealousy**—when a partner attends to others (of either sex) or work or another activity.

- ♥ **In-laws**—the manner of relating to the other's parents.

- ♥ **Chores**—household maintenance, childcare, errands, financial matters.

These major areas of disagreement may be made to 'carry' other behaviours which are felt to be too close to the bone to be tackled directly—lack of affection, abuse, addiction, illness, extra-marital affairs, prior marriages, personal habits, religion, values and expectations.

The behaviours which provoke conflict may vary according to the stage which the relationship has reached, and to whether it is growing or deteriorating. The emphasis of conflict may change between stages, according to whether and how the couple have completed the 'tasks' of each stage. Men and women themselves develop at different rates, and because of this and their innate and cultural differences, they will not view the same behaviours as problems at the same time. We handle conflict differently at different stages, too. Young couples will fight, analyse or joke about issues, and will employ a more direct and expressive style of communication. Middle-aged couples discuss things in a more non-committal and tangential way and can often lack focus. Older couples have either learned to confront issues early before they get to the stage of conflict, or will use avoidance techniques which, with long practice, have become quite sophisticated.

How conflict develops

Since conflict is an inevitable and persistent element in the interaction of husband and wife, it can be seen—like the relationship—as a process which changes and develops, rather than as something static. Conflict progresses through three stages:

♥ the seeds of conflict are sown if the partners are faced with a choice between two or more incompatible options or goals: we cannot go on holiday if your mother is coming to stay; we shall not be able to afford a car if you give up work to have a baby; we can't both go to the party if you don't get a babysitter

♥ the conflict becomes evident when it is revealed that the partners want different things. Blame and accusation follow

♥ the conflict threatens the relationship if the partners do not find a mutually acceptable outcome; one or other must now back down or make a sacrifice in order to resolve the difference. At this point, which is typical of the 'power struggle' stage of marriage, self-interest takes over from mutual interest. Too much is lost by backing down, for the couple are into a 'winners and losers' situation. For some, this stage of conflict may spell the end of the intimacy of the relationship, even of the marriage itself.

A man tends to avoid marital conflict, and one way of doing this is to respond by 'stonewalling' (not replying, avoiding eye contact and not moving or changing facial expressions). Communication is impossible from then on, thereby infuriating his wife, for this physical withdrawal from the arena heralds an emotional withdrawal, and avoidance. She will usually pursue and try to re-engage her husband, and a pattern of escalating advance and withdrawal becomes established, bringing misery, anger and frustration. If the wife counters by withdrawing as well then there is little hope for the couple, who will then be travelling separate, if parallel, roads. Marriages may go on like this for long periods, if not for ever, sometimes physically symbolized by sexual alienation. One man and wife interviewed in counselling managed to live entirely separately at opposite ends of the large country vicarage which was the family home.

Avoidance

We look below at how couples can confront contentious issues and feelings before real damage is done, for this type of conflict evasion can often be fatal to a relationship. However, not all avoidance is bad, for there are some differences which cannot be resolved and which must be tolerated (for example, the problem of elderly relatives). For the sake of the long-term functioning and stability of the relationship it may be better—once all options have been reviewed, *and feelings openly acknowledged*—not to risk direct confrontation. If one partner, for example, is still greatly lacking in trust, or if one has had an affair, the *feelings* of both should be discussed, but the issue itself may be best avoided. But this is definitely not the same as ignoring it.

Conflict resolution

We come to each other in marriage from the depths of our childhood, trailing the experiences and bearing the scars which have formed our personalities, and hoping that the less than perfect bits won't show. These same experiences will fashion our expectations of relationships. Inevitably, sooner or later, we feel a niggling dissatisfaction, we experience a negative feeling—our needs are not being met, our expectations are unfulfilled. This 'pinch' is the beginning of potential conflict within relationship. We can deal with the pinch in one of three ways:

- ignore it and hope it will go away in an attempt not to rock the boat;

- deal with it indirectly, perhaps with a joke, or make up the tiff without talking about it;

- talk it through and renegotiate our expectations.

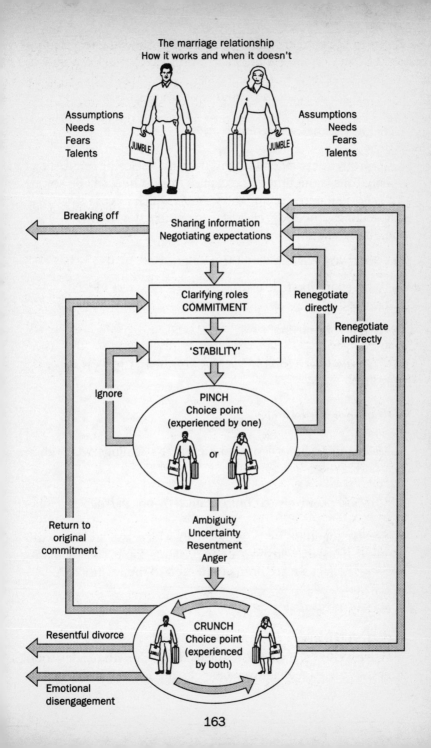

The marriage relationship
How it works and when it doesn't

Assumptions
Needs
Fears
Talents

JUMBLE

Assumptions
Needs
Fears
Talents

JUMBLE

Breaking off

Sharing information
Negotiating expectations

Clarifying roles
COMMITMENT

Renegotiate
directly

Renegotiate
indirectly

'STABILITY'

Ignore

PINCH
Choice point
(experienced by one)

or

JUMBLE

JUMBLE

Return to
original
commitment

Ambiguity
Uncertainty
Resentment
Anger

Resentful divorce

CRUNCH
Choice point
(experienced
by both)

JUMBLE

JUMBLE

Emotional
disengagement

163

These pinches are uncomfortable, but they show the relationship is alive. They can be either pitfalls which lead to its deterioration, or steps to growth. For them to lead to growth and the couple's fitness, we must work through the following sequence:

1. Recognize that something is amiss.

2. Confront our partner with this truth by disclosing our feelings openly. This is the time to be explicit, for nothing will be solved if it is not out in the open. The formula which forces us to 'own' our feelings (nobody else is responsible for them) will be something like this:

- 'When you come in late I feel... because... '

- 'When you don't clear up your mess after you I feel... because... '

- 'When your mother says... I feel... because...'

We must avoid accusations such as 'You always... '; 'You never... '; 'You make me feel... '

3. Challenge without accusing.

4. Listen and acknowledge our partner's feelings when they respond.

5. Respond positively to confrontation by our partner.

6. Search together for a solution in which we are both the winners. This may involve us in making some changes, witnessing the fact we are both committed to the relationship.

7. Set ourselves realistic goals.

Crunch time

We have a choice. If we do not deal effectively with niggles soon after they arise (at whatever stage of marriage), if we just ignore them, try to solve them alone, sacrifice ourselves and soldier on, they will grow and will lead to a far more serious crisis. When this arises both partners will be in no doubt that there is something seriously wrong, for the situation will be ambiguous and uncertain, if not intolerable. Resentment and anger will constantly well up. Communication will be at an all-time low, and each exchange will be newly bruising and painful. At this stage the couple may step back from the brink and decide they must save the relationship. But merely 'forgetting' the past and starting afresh will not work, and the escalating spiral of reproaches and complaints will repeat. Some couples may choose to put a decent façade on a relationship which has died, and many co-exist in this state of cold war for years. Others will head for the divorce courts.

The couple who seriously wish to save their marriage and put it on a new and more stable footing will have to renegotiate, but it is infinitely harder now than when the first pinches were felt. Problems in marriage keep getting larger if not treated, and do not just go away of their own accord. People in healthy relationships face up to issues gently and immediately, and the further the couple are along their journey the more practised they will get.

Counselling

The couple who have reached crisis point, and are unable to renegotiate under this stress because of the high level of conflict, may now seek help from someone with the appropriate skills, such as a marriage counsellor. Often only one will look for this kind of help, and the personal growth which results may mean that the relationship becomes even less satisfactory to both parties. People looking for counselling help should ask, before the process starts, whether the counsellor considers the individuals or the relationship to be the client. There is these days much less determination to save the marriage at all costs; the emphasis is rather on ensuring the couple take responsibility themselves for their decision to continue the marriage, or to end it.

Counselling helps people by providing them with a safe relationship (with the counsellor) in which they can explore their situation, discover their hidden feelings and gain greater insight that will help them deal more effectively with their lives. It can be the opportunity for couples to learn the necessary communication and problem-solving skills, which ideally should have been absorbed at an early age by observation of parents who put these into practice.

The earlier these skills are learned the better, for marriages, like people, get set in their ways quickly and easily, and it is difficult to unlearn old and unproductive ways of interacting. Couples must learn the rules and boundaries for making their conflict creative and for managing conflict within both the relationship *and themselves*. Individual counselling may help a person 'find themselves', but it is only when their behaviour and their interactions can be seen in the context of the couple (or the family system) that real changes can be made in the relationship. It will often require only a tiny shift within it for the whole thing to become unstuck and move forward again. We look at communication in more detail in the next chapter.

The end of the road?

Hilary and Alec

After a passionate romance, Hilary, now thirty-four, had married Alec, who was fifty, while she was still at university where he was a lecturer. She was flattered by his constant attentiveness, though she was never invited to meet his friends. As time went by, Alec built up serious debts and his drinking habits became a cause for concern. Hilary worked hard to pay off the debts, but he remained bitter and sarcastic about the work she did. Lately he had been hitting her and causing severe bruising.

He came to the first counselling session only, and Hilary continued alone. With the counsellor's help she gradually came to the realization that she had seen Alec as a substitute for her father, who had died when she was four. His attentions had blinded her to his less likeable ways.

Hilary's confidence grew, and despite (or perhaps because of) her new-found assertiveness, her husband grew more morose and violent. Although she thought she still loved him at times, she ended her counselling knowing she could face the future without him.

When couples are unable to resolve conflict they feel badly about both the issues and themselves, and they begin to develop doubts about each other and the relationship that can lead ultimately to disengagement. They may at this time decide to separate and the marriage may end.

Recent proposals for divorce law reform are an attempt to ensure that divorce is not so easy that husband and wife have no incentive to learn to overcome difficulties and try to resolve conflict; for with help, resolution is possible even at breakdown stage if both partners want to try. The objectives of the British Parliamentary White Paper, published in April 1995, were:

♥ to support the institution of marriage;

♥ to include practical steps to prevent the irretrievable breakdown of marriage;

♥ to ensure the parties understand the consequences of divorce in advance;

♥ to minimize the bitterness and hostility between the couple and minimize the trauma for the children;

♥ to keep costs to a minimum.

If these proposals become law, parting couples will be expected—though not obliged—to use mediation to sort out property and children. Here is the assessment, as recorded in the *Daily Telegraph* on 28 April 1995, of one divorcing couple who had used conjoint mediation (a male and female counsellor working in a foursome with the couple) in such circumstances:

Wife: I discovered a lot about what was happening in my husband's life through mediation... Initially, that was horrifying, but once everything was out, it could be dealt with. I used the sessions as a counselling service... For example, I was very upset over the manner in which James took his furniture, but I waited until the mediation session to say so.

Husband: *It was the unexpected things that cropped up in the course of conversation that brought home how far the marriage breakdown had gone. Some things came up which, in a letter, would have sent you screaming into orbit. It was sometimes painful, sometimes frustrating, but always worthwhile enough to go on.*

Their conclusion was that:

Husband: *I can't say that we have come out of this best buddies—we still have a lot of emotional baggage to deal with—but we have to be in touch over the children and we can communicate now, whereas we couldn't before.*

The result here was that both ex-partners learned a great deal about themselves and consequently gained the capacity to be better parents, and possibly better spouses should they ever consider marrying again. Divorce—although it may ultimately bring relief and peace—is almost always agony, with all the consequences of loss and grief for the man, the woman, and for their children. Being helped to know ourselves through this process may mean that something positive can come of the huge negation of personal value and worth that divorce can bring.

If both partners decide that their marriage is effectively unsavable, it is once again the *process* by which decisions are arrived at which will determine whether, even in the face of breakdown, we can learn more of ourselves, grow and move forward on our individual journey.

Conflict as a step to growth

We have seen that conflict shows that a marriage is alive and ready to move forward. It is not necessarily destructive if the process of resolving it uses the couple's communication skills, prompts them to a deeper disclosure of their feelings (thus revealing more of their true selves), leads them to listen non-defensively to the other, and is handled positively with empathy and the other great balm of married life—humour. It is often more the nature of the interaction than its result which restores intimacy and mutual satisfaction.

CHAPTER 13

Communication: a New Attitude

DIALOGUE, ROLES, SEX

Communication is to a relationship as oxygen is to the brain. Without communication, there is irreparable damage and the relationship will die—or continue in a lifeless shell, brain-dead, sustained artificially for form's sake. If you cannot communicate your real self to me, I shall not know who you are. If I cannot communicate myself to you I shall not see the reflection of my true self in you. Without communication we could survive on fantasy for a while, but it would be like living on a diet of chocolate bars.

Despite our yearnings for intimacy, to know and be known, communication is not something innate but a skill to be learned and practised. Our style of communicating, or our difficulties in doing so, will be absorbed initially by observing our parents' model. Did our parents share their thoughts and feelings with each other? How? Did they sit down and talk in the kitchen or living room, or did they withdraw behind closed doors in the bedroom? Did we hear rows? Did one sulk? Did the other rage?

Peter: I just remember being frightened every night. I'd lie in bed and shiver and hear them scream at each other. I thought they'd kill each other. I don't even want to remember the house where we lived when I was little, specially not my bedroom where I could hear them from at night.

In Peter's own marriage there were never any rows, nor communication other than superficial domestic exchange, and after a while no sex either. Peter had become a cold, withdrawn and distant man whose fear of closeness had been formed during those evenings listening to the tempest of his parents' non-communication.

If we can begin to reveal our real emotions, the truth of ourselves to our partner, then the relationship will benefit:

♥ we shall not be hiding anything behind a mask, so we shall feel more comfortable

♥ we can focus on the problem in hand rather than use our energy to be 'right'

♥ we can use our creative imagination in solving the problem rather than in defending ourselves

♥ we can work out solutions to problems on the basis of the real issues involved rather than addressing the façades

♥ we can reveal openly both our selfishness and our loving concern and let these conflicting desires find an acceptable balance

♥ we can freely change and grow, without being bound by the rigidity of 'should', 'ought' and 'must'

♥ we shall be perceived as more genuine, and the other will be less suspicious of what may lie beneath our façade

♥ this trust will in turn invite openness and reality from the other.

You're a selfish pig and you're never ever on time and I hate you!

It is evident that such a statement will produce neither change nor growth, for it will induce defensiveness and dissimulation and says nothing about the reality of the accuser or the accused.

Genuine and open communication would go something like this:

I feel anxious and apprehensive and unloved when you're back after the time you said, because all sorts of black thoughts go through my head about what you might be doing or what might have happened.

The American therapist, Carl Rogers, writes in his book, *On Becoming a Person*:

Each person is an island unto himself, in a very real sense; and he can only build bridges to other islands if he is first of all willing to be himself and permitted to be himself. [35]

Communication means simply being ourselves with the other person. It means not acting as though we were something we are not, a stratagem which demands energy and reduces our effectiveness as people.

However, to be ourselves implies first that we must accept ourselves as we are. If we can do this we shall be secure enough in ourselves to go out to meet the other, to receive their reality, to accept it, to understand and to empathize. And in entering into another's reality we shall be enriched and changed. If in our personal developmental journey we have not learned to trust ourselves or others, then the first 'romance' stage of marriage will be vital in giving us the chance to catch up on what we missed in infancy.

This is the lifelong work of marriage, but it has a particular significance for the new couple who are emerging from their dream of romance *à deux*. It is at this stage in their journey that it is enormously difficult to permit the other to think or feel differently about problems or issues. Yet, in the words of Carl Rogers again:

... this separateness of individuals, the right of each individual to utilize his experience in his own way and to discover his own meanings in it—this is one of the most priceless potentialities of life.

The feelings that the real self attempts to transmit when it communicates in intimacy with another will be either positive or negative. Positive feelings (the 'affective affirmation' we looked at in the Postscript to Part II) would include love, admiration, tenderness, warmth; negative feelings would include jealousy, shame, anger, sadness, irritation or fear. Being sweetly reasonable while seething with fury underneath is not acting with integrity. We shall be our real selves if we can express our anger and explain its cause. When we learn to express these emotions genuinely, we 'own' them as part of ourselves; we demonstrate our knowledge that they are not caused by another, and we drop our defensive mask. As Rogers says, it is 'as though the map of expression of feelings has come to match more closely the territory of the actual emotional experience'.

This is communication. It is living a relationship on the basis of truth, trusting that the world and the relationship will not come to an end. It is accepting that we have needs, fears, griefs, expectations, hopes, joys, frustrations—and speaking them out. Without this two-way trust the marriage cannot move on its journey through the inevitable difficulties ahead. The following, from the *Daily Telegraph* of 25 November 1994, is an extreme example of what happens when this basic trust and communication are not achieved:

She can still remember the feeling of the bolt as it struck her skull... then turning round and seeing her husband standing there, a crossbow in his shaking hands. As the blood began pumping, she recalls looking at it, and raising her hand to pull out the black, pointed dart lodged behind her ear. The jealousy her husband felt about her achievements as a programme manager had intensified to the point where he wanted to kill her...

He [had become] *overpoweringly possessive. 'If I was five minutes late picking the boys up from the childminder, he would accuse me of having an affair. In my field most of my colleagues are men. He could not cope with that... I would sit shaking on the train if I was late. I knew what to expect. He would grab me round the neck, push me up against the wall and hiss terrible, terrible things at me.'*

There were doubtless other, psychological factors at play in Barry Kirby's obsessive attacks on his professionally successful wife Terry, but the story serves as an example of the potentially fatal frustrations which build up if a person cannot acknowledge and accept their emotions, and in trust communicate the reality of them to their spouse. Mr Kirby put an unbearable pressure on his wife to have the same feelings as he did, not to be a separate person. In other words he was unwilling to let go of the 'romance' stage where the lovers are fused in a blissful union with eyes only for each other. His behaviour was shrieking, 'If you want my love, you must feel the same as I do. Your behaviour is bad and you must feel so too.'

Our willingness to let our partner be separate and unique, with individual values and activities, witnesses to our *personal* maturity; while the ability to be separate, with separate goals, and yet bound together by the feelings that exist between us is, as we have seen, a sign of *relational* maturity.

The skills of communication

Listen to me, do but listen, and let that be the comfort you offer me.

Job 21:2 (New English Bible)

Intimate relationships depend for their depth on the exposure and sharing of vulnerability. If our relationship is to thrive rather than degenerate then we need to become what these days is called 'emotionally literate', which is a way of saying we need to know what the truth of our feelings is and communicate it accurately. This is the only way of transforming the fantasy of a marriage, or any relationship, into reality.

Because becoming a couple is such a complex process, the husband and wife must become aware of the way they interact, how and what they share with each other, and how they listen and respond. They will need to learn the behaviours which will deflect or decrease conflict, and they need to practise the sort of discussion that focuses on resolving a problem rather than name-calling and blaming. What ideally should come to us from

174

our parents is a sequence of three steps, which if learned young will not be a conscious process:

♥ identify which behaviour gives positive and which gives negative results

♥ alter the pattern of responses to each other to produce a positive result

♥ assess, evaluate and maintain these behavioural patterns.

If our parental model did not teach us these steps by example, then they have to be part of a conscious and voluntary learning process between partners. We will have to learn to verbalize and negotiate productive responses to use when differences emerge and conflict threatens. This means being both kind, but also open and honest, about behaviour which produces a negative response. 'You make me feel furious/guilty/sick/inadequate' will tend to provoke and sustain a row (and anyway, no one else *makes* us feel anything), while 'I feel angry/sad/at a loss/unable to cope' will contribute positively to the reality of the relationship.

All this is hard to remember if we are wounded and snarling, so the mechanisms must be agreed and put in place from the start. And that requires both a recognition that the romantic glow will dim, and a conscious will to communicate and confront problems right from the beginning.

The specific skills we need are:

♥ self-disclosure—'When you do this... I feel... ' (for example: threatened, bad, unwanted, humiliated; or— accepted, great, better, on top of the world)

♥ listening and feedback—can we reflect back accurately what our partner has just said to us?

♥ empathy—do we capture and understand the feeling behind it as well?

♥ negotiating—do we turn ambiguous or negative niggles (the 'pinches') into specific, constructive, positive suggestions?

♥ revealing hidden agendas—are we aware of, and able to make explicit, previously unstated issues which relate to the relationship, our needs, wants, expectations, hopes and fears?

♥ reading non-verbal signs—are we conscious of our own and our spouse's means of body language, what it signifies and the effect it has on the other?

If we can do all this our marriage will gain in warmth, closeness and trust. Even our love-life will improve, for exactly the same skills are required in sexual communication.

If we cannot do this, then our relationship can slide into negativity, mutual abuse, reduced marital satisfaction and sometimes physical violence—an extreme of non-verbal communication born of the frustration of not being able to tell our partner the reality about ourselves.

We need to remember, too, in the hassle of juggling professional and domestic routines, and in the hurly-burly of young parenthood, that we need time to be with each other, to plan, talk, discuss... and be.

Putting it into practice

Sit down and take a few minutes with your partner to complete the following sentences each, an exercise taken from Margaret Grimer's book, *Making Marriage Work*. Do them spontaneously without reflecting too long on the answers. Remember there is no right or wrong way of doing it, for you are communicating your real self.

● Something I don't like about myself is...

● I feel hurt when...

● I'm jealous when...

● I daydream that...

● When you disagree with me I...

● I'm really happy when...

- I get angry if...

- I am scared of...

- Something I'm a bit ashamed of is...

- I wish I were able to...

- It makes me excited when...

- I've often wanted to tell you that...

The golden rules of communicating your real self:

- Be generous in doing it.

- Use it appropriately in terms of the moment and the place.

- Don't save it up and dump it on your spouse.

- Share your reactions to events as they happen.

- Talk about feelings as well as events.

- Take risks in order to be understood at a deeper level.

- Be honest in return to your partner's self-disclosure.

- Try to be courteous—don't use communication in order to wound someone else.

- Expect your knowledge of the reality of yourselves and your partner to deepen.

Roles

Our expectations of what husbands and wives are form a large part of the fantasy which may typify the early months of marriage. Our original models for marriage were our parents, but perhaps we came from a one-parent family or had a stepfather or stepmother. We shall have observed the marriages of our friends' parents when we were young, and perhaps now some of our friends will be living in their own marriages and committed relationships. We may have been influenced, to a greater or lesser degree, by the precepts of feminism; we may be determined to be a New Man, or conversely to be macho and 'not stand any nonsense'! Here are some young husbands quoted by Mansfield and Collard in *The Beginning of the Rest of Your Life?*:

I follow my dad—it was always the wife who cooked the meals and did the ironing and did the vacuum cleaning and washed the kitchen floor and I do all the decorating because they're the more masculine jobs.

You expect your wife to be the same as your mother... but you have a rude awakening.

I say I've got no shirts left, whereas I would never have to with me mum—I'd go to the cupboard and there'd be a shirt there.

This role stereotyping does still happen. And young women still collude with it. On the other hand, a woman may have definite ideas on pursuing her career—children or not—which she will expect her husband to fit in with.

In my mother's day women were happy to stop work when they had children and to live second-hand through their husbands. To the modern woman, who is as well qualified as her partner and used to her own income, the idea is anathema.
Sally Holloway, *Daily Telegraph*, 30 December 1994

A connected article by Cassandra Jardine proclaimed:

The cherished female belief that they are best at looking after children is being whittled away. Not only do men seem as good at changing nappies and building Duplo; they seem to take it in their stride, seeing it as a job rather than a vocation, which makes it emotionally less draining.

With traditional, familial and contemporary interpretations of these roles often at variance, the couple starting out on their journey must make it a priority to clarify the values which make them wish to adopt particular roles as husband and wife. Expectations arising from these may be extremely high, and the frustration when these are not met correspondingly great. If there is genuine communication at the beginning, and throughout the marriage (and roles will be a source of debate and potential conflict at the transition point to every new stage of marriage), then many of the pitfalls on the road ahead can be avoided.

It will take effort and perseverance to get round these snakes, many of which took up their positions during the centuries before our birth. However, talking freely and honestly about our childhood and our families, and communicating and negotiating our expectations of our own relationship and household, will turn potential snakes into ladders of growth together.

Sex—the ultimate body language

Researcher: How do you resolve quarrels between you?

Wife: In bed... [laughs]... *you asked!*

Husband: I would say in the time we've married and we've been in the same house there is one night when I slept on the sofa, and that was only for about two hours till Pat came and joined me, and I would say only about thirteen nights that we've gone to sleep without 'saying goodnight'—I mean touching each other.

Wife: That's a very strong part, I think. A friend once said, 'I can see what makes your marriage work.' But it's a part of the whole thing, it's not over-riding everything else.

Husband: My mother-in-law gives up her bed for visitors and sleeps on a settee. We've always said, haven't we, 'We give up our bed for nobody.' We won't give up our bed. I believe that's sacrosanct. At my house, I mean, my parents' room was sacrosanct, if the door was shut.

This couple from the research sample had been married for more than thirty years, and had always found that, although they said sex was not 'the whole part' of their marriage, it was a valued, valid, and sometimes vital form of communication when words were not quite safe enough to be trusted after a breakdown of communication.

Sex is the ultimate non-verbal communication, the language of the body which, although it can never replace the verbal conveying of feeling, is a powerful force of communication within the marriage. The psychiatrist Dr Jack Dominian sums up this aspect of sexual intercourse:

> *It is not easy to be available, to communicate effectively, to show affection, and to negotiate conflict without a constant supply of energy and encouragement which sexual intercourse gives... Responding to the wounded part of our partner is often dealing with the irritable, angry, impatient, impulsive, intolerant, generally difficult part of our spouse.* [36]

Sexual love is also, and significantly, an example of how couples, even if married for decades, can legitimately 'redo' an early stage of the marriage, for sex takes us right back to the days of 'romance', when we had eyes only for each other, were fused in an ecstatic oneness, talking the private—often inarticulated—language of lovers, and the rest of the world didn't exist. Sex is a return to this, even if afterwards we have to get up and face everyday reality again.

Christopher Clulow says more bluntly, 'Intercourse in bed normally reflects intercourse out of bed,' meaning that the place of sex in the marriage will most often mirror the quality of the couple's communication out of bed. Both sexual and verbal communication within the committed relationship could rightly be called 'making love', for both require that the partners make themselves available to each other, explore the world through each other's eyes, and learn their emotional language.

Sexual intimacy and communication both require us to drop our defences, to be 'naked', and thus vulnerable. As in all aspects of marriage there is a perceptual gulf between men and women as regards their sexuality, and this can be a path to discord and bitterness. In the film *Annie Hall*, Woody Allen tells his psychiatrist that he and Annie have sex 'hardly ever, maybe three times a week'. Annie tells her shrink that they do it 'constantly; I'd say three times a week'—which suggests that sex is indeed a microcosm of the whole relationship, in which there is always *his* reality and *her* reality (see Chapter 12).

A study of sex in the United States published in 1994 bears out this difference of gender in the perception of sexuality.[37] For example, 54 per cent of men in the study say they think about sex every day or several times a day. By contrast, 67 per cent of the women say they think about it only a few times a week or a few times a month. This 'disconnect' is even greater when it comes to 'forced sex'. According to the report, 22 per cent of women say they have been forced to do sexual things they didn't want to, usually by someone they loved. But only 3 per cent of men admit to ever forcing themselves on women. It would thus appear that men and women have somewhat different ideas on what constitutes voluntary sex.

In sex, as in other forms of marital communication, expectations and feelings should be exchanged openly and honestly. It is an area where wounds can go deep, and it is all the more vital to avoid, 'You never... ' or 'Why can't you... ?' The same formulae as in verbal communication skills apply to sex: 'When you do that I feel... because... ' When we can do this we are transmitting the reality of ourselves to the other.

Love is shown in many ways. The principal one is an act of sharing, and the depth and range of our sharing will reflect our commitment to each other. What we are sharing is our true self—emotionally, psychologically, mentally, spiritually and physically. The way we share is by communicating genuinely and openly. If we withhold our true selves, and withdraw from each other, we are diminished, love is diminished, the relationship is diminished. Conversely, if we begin to trust the other with ourselves we come to know more of the depths of our own being, and thus have more of ourselves available to communicate.

Conclusion

Good enough?[35]

In the course of researching this book, many marriage and relationships counsellors were consulted. These were men and women whose own marriages had, for the most part, endured for between twenty and forty years. Yet the general feeling was that the tasks of each stage of marriage involve blood, sweat, toil and tears. The journey through marriage, they said, is not easy; few start with the emotional and psychological fitness to succeed, or the stamina to keep working when things are difficult.

When pressed to define what 'success' might mean, the consensus was that it was much more than staying together. It implied an ongoing relationship which enabled one eventually to become, and to be, one's true self. When it worked it was enriching, but the path was a difficult one and some fell by the wayside. The counsellors had witnessed much pain, much tearing apart, much bitterness. A significant proportion of the interviews themselves did not yield much more cause for optimism. A handful of couples did, however, demonstrate aspects of the last two stages of 'working it through' and 'collaboration'. And one of these had had to find their way through the stress and distress of the wife's extra-marital relationship. It can be done.

A frequently recurring issue to emerge from case studies was the amount of physical violence between couples. There is no way of knowing whether this is increasing; there has always been domestic violence and perhaps it is only that people, especially women, are now freer and more willing to disclose it. Heavy drinking was also a feature of case material. Both behaviours testify to the pain and frustration of those trapped in marriages that may be going nowhere and which bring nothing.

Such patterns also show that when expectations of relationships are high, disappointment and bitterness can follow. This may explain why increasing numbers of people are now actually choosing to live on their own, sporadically taking up what may be called 'free unions'—sexual relationships without any commitment other than a fleeting engagement of time, and little else. The following newspaper commentary followed a report that fewer people are now living in couples, let alone marrying.

> *Free, free as air... no thanks, not this evening—I've got a date with myself. Free to be intoxicated by freedom without spreading my wings. Free to go out or to stay in. Free to vegetate wiggling my toes in front of the TV, free not to watch it if I don't want to. Free to read, to smoke, to dream. Free not to do the chores. Free as a bachelor. Free as a bird in a tree since it's my tree and no one else's. And even free, at last free, not to answer all those unasked questions.*
>
> Translated from *Le Monde*, 6 July 1995

To which could be added—free never to know the depths of another being, free never to see myself reflected in the other, free not to grow and develop, free not to carve out my true identity from the rockface of relationship, but free indeed not to know conflict, free always to avoid the issues which I find uncomfortable.

The day this book was being completed, the Family Policy Studies Centre published an article in their *Family Policy Bulletin*, July 1995 called 'Making Marriage Work', underlining the fact that more people are choosing to cohabit or live alone rather than marry, with the result that the marriage rate is now at its lowest level for fifty years. It therefore called for an investigation of the declining status of marriage and ways of providing financial help to enable couples to stay together. The accompanying press release by Ceridwen Roberts stated:

> *A proper analysis of the benefits of supporting prevention* [of marital breakdown] *against the costs of picking up the pieces needs to be undertaken. It is important to show cohabiting breakdown, not just marriages.*

We just do not know enough about what makes marriages work and what to do to help people at an early enough stage. Unless we back up our calls for more responsibility in relationships with a clearer understanding of why things go wrong, and with resources to help people, we will continue to have increasing levels of divorce and fewer committed relationships.

The author of this book listened to many couples, some bitter and bewildered at a painful or a past relationship, some grateful but equally uncomprehending as to why they had shared half a lifetime of fulfilling, though not necessarily easy, marriage. One of the latter, married some 32 years, said it was a combination of 'luck, lust and love'. But it is certain that a 'good' marriage is more than merely the sum of its component parts, and it is doubtless easier to analyse failure than success.

In attempting to explore committed couple relationship at the end of the twentieth century, and the emotional muscle required to work at it, the author has frequently had recourse to the opinions of the pundits of the press and magazine world; but they too seem baffled at what makes a 'good' marriage.

This book is a contribution to the understanding of why and how some marriages 'work' and some do not, and it has attempted to show that 'luck' has very little to do with the selection of a mate and the undertaking of the journey together which is marriage. A good marriage—one that makes us happy and which spreads this happiness beyond the family circle—is not just the result of luck, either. Instead of saying 'when it works', we should perhaps train ourselves to say 'when *we* work', for success will depend on what work we are prepared to do, what tasks we are prepared to accomplish to create this entity called a couple. For some, it is a long hard road, and there is no let-up in the effort; this is especially so for those who are handicapped by the wounds of childhood and weighed down with the baggage of early life. For others, though, the prospect is easier—more a question, as elderly couples so often point out, of 'give and take'.

And we do have that choice: whether to turn tail and run, dig into some cosy corner never to come out—or to go on learning and growing, examining issues, facing conflict, communicating the reality of ourselves to each other. Marriage can 'work'. Naturally, there will be problems; the marriage would be dull indeed without them! But the message of this book is that difficulties in marriage are opportunities to learn more about ourselves and our partner, and that they are learning experiences rather than grounds for divorce. It can be the process of resolving contentious issues rather than their outcome which gives the most satisfaction, deepens knowledge and promotes growth.

If couples can view marriage as a journey that is undertaken in stages that unfold before them as they progress, then they may find hope in the distress of the moment and they may have less anxiety about their future. They will find in it an agenda for sorting out their differences and problems, the niggles and the pinches.

But it would be naïve and short-sighted to believe that *every* marriage can survive, let alone be rich and fruitful. Sometimes our wounds are too deep, our capacity for love too limited, to be able travel long distances in relationship with another, and it is inescapable that there are marriages which will fail. In these cases it is possible that a second attempt at matrimony, if we have found the potential for healing and growth, will succeed. If not, a second marriage—as statistics demonstrate—will be more likely than the first to break down.

No marriage can be constantly and euphorically happy over the years. If we grasp and assimilate this, it may enable us to let go of our concept of instant happy-ever-afterness, of a childish desire for gratification *now*. We must understand that both we ourselves and our relationships are constantly changing, and will require flexibility, modification, evolution and redesigning. In other words, the landscape is different at every step on our journey and we must adapt with it. We must be 'developmentally mobile'.

The will to travel together through marriage, to make things work out—if it is strong enough in both partners—can redeem all the fragilities. For this to happen will require awareness, vulnerability and above all communication of the truth of ourselves. Then, maybe, we shall have created a marriage that is not merely 'good enough', but one of which we may be proud.

Footnotes

1   Christopher Clulow and Janet Mattinson, *Marriage Inside Out*, Pelican Books, 1989.

2   The Joseph Rowntree Foundation, *Family and parenthood. Supporting families, preventing breakdown*, 1995.

3   Penny Mansfield and Jean Collard, *The Beginning of the Rest of Your Life*, Macmillan Press, 1988.

4   John Haskey, 'Premarital cohabitation and the probability of subsequent divorce', *Population Trends* 68, pp 10-19.

5   Pope Pius XI, *Casti Connubii*, 1957.

6   Cardinal Hume, *The Tablet*, 27 August 1994.

7   *Cosmopolitan*, US edition, January 1995.

8   *Cosmopolitan*, US edition, January 1995.

9   *Cosmopolitan*, US edition, January 1995.

10 Petronella Wyatt, *The Sunday Telegraph*, 11 September 1994.

11 A. Stevenson, *Archetype: a Natural History of the Self*

12 From J. Luft, *Group Processes: an introduction to group dynamics*, National Press, Palo Alto, California, 1966.

13 Edward Blishen, *The Penny World*, Sinclair-Stevenson, 1990.

14 Liberty Kovacs, 'Couple Therapy: an integrated developmental and family systems model', *Family Therapy*, 15(2), 1988.

15 Edward Blishen, *The Penny World*, Sinclair-Stevenson, 1990.

16 Mary Kirk and Tom Leary, *Holy Matrimony? An exploration of marriage and ministry*, Lynx Communications, 1994.

17 Lawrence Kohlberg, *The Philosophy of Moral Development*, Harper and Row, San Francisco, 1981.

18 Carol Gilligan, *In a Different Voice*, Harvard University Press, 1982/93.

19 Office of Population Censuses and Surveys figures suggest that women are increasingly delaying the start of a family till after they are thirty. The proportion is rising sharply, and it is predicted that more than one-third of women born in 1967 will still be childless at thirty. Furthermore, twice as many women in 1991 as in 1986 said that they expected to remain childless.

20 The developmental sequence of marriage described here was developed and formalized mainly by Liberty Kovaks in the United States, and the diagram of the stages adapted from one

designed by Deirdre Morrod, training officer of One Plus One, the marriage and partnership research charity.

21 From *Social Trends* 25, Central Statistical Office, based on the latest figures available (1992).

22 Erich Fromm, *Escape from Freedom*.

23 *Cosmopolitan*, US edition, January 1995.

24 John Powell SJ, *The Secret of Staying in Love*, Tabor Press, 1974.

25 Reprinted in the *Weekly Telegraph* of 25 April 1995.

26 *Cosmopolitan*, US edition, January 1995.

27 Quoted by Liberty Kovaks in workshop material.

28 Gordon Lowe, *The Growth of Personality*, Pelican Books, 1972.

29 Liberty Kovaks, quoted in *The Sacramento Bee*, 16 February 1992.

30 Robin Skynner and John Cleese, *Life and How to Survive It*, Methuen, 1993.

31 John Powell SJ, *The Secret of Staying in Love*, Tabor Press, 1974.

32 By the humanistic psychologist Abraham Maslow (1908–70).

33 From the Institute for Social Research, University of Michigan, Ann Arbor, 1989–95.

34 John Gottman, quoted in H.E. Marano, 'The Reinvention of Marriage', *Psychology Today*, Jan/Feb 1992.

35 Carl Rogers, *On Becoming a Person, A Therapist's View of Psychotherapy*, Constable, 1961.

36 Jack Dominian, *Passionate and Compassionate Love*, Darton, Longman and Todd, 1991.

37 Edward Laumann *et al*, *The Social Organization of Sexuality*, University of Chicago, 1994.

Index

Text Acknowledgments

We are grateful to all those who have given us permission to quote material used in this book. Every effort has been made to trace and contact copyright holders. If there are any inadvertent omissions or errors in the acknowledgments we apologize to those concerned.

Introduction
p16: Reproduced by permission of Penguin Books Ltd, from *Marriage Inside Out*, Christopher Clulow and Janet Mattinson, Pelican.

Chapter 1
p25: Extracts from *The Book of Common Prayer*, the rights in which are vested in the Crown, are reproduced by permission of the Crown's Patentee, Cambridge University Press.
Material from *The Alternative Service Book 1980* is copyright © The Central Board of Finance of the Church of England and is reproduced by permission.
pp26, 30, 33: From *The Independent on Sunday*/Janet Watts, 21 November 1993.
pp26, 37: From *The Beginning of the Rest of Your Life*, Penny Mansfield and Jean Collard, 1988, by permission of Macmillan Ltd.
p27: Reproduced by permission of The Church Union, 7 Tufton Street, London SW1P 3QN, from *Living Stones*/Martin Dudley.
p28: © The Telegraph plc, London, 1995.
pp32/33, 36: From *The Tablet*, The International Catholic Weekly/Cardinal Basil Hume, 27 August 1994.
p34: Constable & Co. Ltd, from *One Flesh, Separate Persons*, Robin Skynner.
p35: Darton, Longman and Todd, from *Man and Woman He Made Them*, Jean Vanier.

Chapter 2
pp41, 44: From *Cosmopolitan*, US edition, January 1995, p70, by permission of Beth Sherman.
p44: © The Telegraph plc, London, 1994.
p46: From *The Times*, 25 March 1995, by permission of Gerald Kaufman.
p47: From *The Times*, 20 January 1995, by permission of A.P. Watt on behalf of Libby Purves.
p53: The Johari Window diagram from *Group Processes: An Introduction to Group Dynamics* by Joseph Luft. Copyright © 1984, 1970, 1969 by Joseph Luft. Reproduced by permission of Mayfield Publishing Co.
p59: From *The Penny World*, Edward Blishen, Sinclair-Stevenson.

Chapter 4
p80: © The Telegraph plc, London, 1994.

Chapter 5
p83: From *The Beginning of the Rest of Your Life*, Penny Mansfield and Jean Collard, 1988, by permission of Macmillan Ltd.

Chapter 6
p97: From *The Beginning of the Rest of Your Life*, Penny Mansfield and Jean Collard, 1988, by permission of Macmillan Ltd.
p101: From *Cosmopolitan*, US edition, January 1995, p76, by permission of Beth Sherman.

p103: Tabor Publishing, from *The Secret of Staying in Love*, John Powell SJ.
© The Telegraph plc, London, 1995.
p105: From *Cosmopolitan*, US edition, January 1995, p78, by permission of Beth Sherman.

Chapter 7
p108: From *The Independent*/Jack Dominian, 27 April 1995.

Chapter 8
p118: Reproduced by permission of Penguin Books Ltd, from *The Growth of Personality*, Gordon Lowe, Pelican.
p121: Reproduced by permission of Penguin Books Ltd, from *Marriage Inside Out*, Christopher Clulow and Janet Mattinson, Pelican.

Chapter 9
pp128/29: This excerpt first appeared in 'Till Divorce Us Do Part', by John Sedgwick, published in Options Magazine
p134: © Christina Hardyment/The Telegraph plc, London, 1995.
p136: © The Telegraph plc, London, 1994.

Chapter 10
p140: From *Life and How to Survive It*, Robin Skynner and John Cleese, (Methuen 1993), by permission of David Wilkinson Associates.

Chapter 11
p144: Tabor Publishing, from *The Secret of Staying in Love*, John Powell SJ.
pp128/29: This excerpt first appeared in 'Till Divorce Us Do Part', by John Sedgwick, published in Options Magazine

Chapter 12
p153: Chatto & Windus, from *Still Life*, by permission of Peters Fraser & Dunlop on behalf of A.S. Byatt.
p166: © The Telegraph plc, London, 1995.
p167: The Marriage Relationship diagram from *Making Marriage Work*, Margaret Grimer, CMAC/Cassell.

Chapter 13
p172: Constable & Co. Ltd, from *On Becoming a Person, A Therapist's View of Psychotherapy*, Carl Rogers, 1961, London.
pp173/74: © The Telegraph plc, London, 1994.
pp176/77: From *Making Marriage Work*, Margaret Grimer, CMAC/Cassell.
p178: From *The Beginning of the Rest of Your Life*, Penny Mansfield and Jean Collard, 1988, by permission of Macmillan Ltd.
p178: From *The Daily Telegraph*, 30 December 1994, by permission of Sally Holloway.
p178: From *The Daily Telegraph*/Cassandra Jardine, 27 December 1994.
p180: Darton, Longman and Todd, from *Passionate and Compassionate Love*, Jack Dominian.

Conclusion
p183: From *Le Monde*, 6 July 1995.
pp183/84: From press release of the Family Policy Studies Centre, Ceridwen Roberts, by permission.